S0-AHV-764

OR · PLAN ·
EVATION

728-3   77990

September
1996

·SCALE · FOR · PLAN ɬ ELEVATION ·

NOTE:
FOLLOWING · ISSUE · OF ·
THE · MONOGRAPH · SERIES ·
WILL · CONTAIN · MEASURED ·
DRAWINGS · OF · THE · INTERIOR ·
OF · THE · BRICE · HOUSE ·.

MEAS ɬ DRAWN · KENNETH CLARK ·

E V A T I O N ·   · S E C T I O N ·

E · H O U S E ·

M A R Y L A N D ·

EARLY ARCHITECTURE
OF RHODE ISLAND

EARLY ARCHITECTURE OF RHODE ISLAND

From material originally published as
The White Pine Series of Architectural Monographs
edited by
Russell F. Whitehead and Frank Chouteau Brown

Lisa C. Mullins, Editor

Roy Underhill, Consultant

A Publication of
THE NATIONAL HISTORICAL SOCIETY

Library of Congress Cataloging-in-Publication Data

Early architecture of Rhode Island.
    (Architectural treasures of early America; 6)
    1. Architecture, Domestic — Rhode Island.   2. Architecture, Colonial — Rhode Island.   3. Architecture, Georgian — Rhode Island.   I. Mullins, Lisa C.
II. Underhill, Roy.   III. Series: Architectural treasures of Early America (Harrisburg, Pa.); 6.
NA7235.R4E16   1988   728.3'7'09745   87-14214
ISBN 0-918678-25-0

The original photographs reproduced in this publication are from the collection of drawings and photographs in "The White Pine Monograph Series, Collected and Edited by Russell F. Whitehead, The George P. Lindsay Collection." The collection, part of the research and reference collections of The American Institute of Architects, Washington, D.C., was acquired by the Institute in 1955 from the Whitehead estate, through the cooperation of Mrs. Russell F. Whitehead, and the generosity of the Weyerhauser Timber Company, which purchased the collection for presentation to the Institute. The research and reference collections of the Institute are available for public use. A written request for such use is required so that space may be reserved and assistance made available.

CONTENTS

THE COLONIAL CURE

It was a culture in shock. The horror of the Civil War was a lingering trauma. The first great waves of non-English-speaking immigrants, searching for their own versions of the American dream, were spreading through the land. Industrialization was attacking the old values, taking traditional crafts (and people) out of the homes and into the factories. The Colonial Revival movement, sparked by the Philadelphia Centennial of 1876, was just what the troubled young country needed.

The Colonial Revival provided a common identity, shared values and a healing national mythology that could coexist with the American ideal of the rugged individual. Rhode Island is the perfect place to study this contradiction in the national character. Rhode Island was created by such independent types as Roger Williams, who escaped the wrath of the Massachusetts magistrates to found Providence in 1636. Two years later, Anne Huchinson and her followers similarly founded Portsmouth. Their homes reflected their individualism. The "stone-ender" houses, such as the Eleazer Arnold House of Lincoln, Rhode Island, shown in Chapter 13, are found nowhere else.

Rhode Island, however, was also one of the first states to suffer the pressures of progress. Samuel Slater's early contributions to the technology of cloth manufacture spawned the growth of the mill towns shown in Chapter 12. As the land was settled, malcontents could no longer just move away. The only physical escape was home, the only spiritual escape was to the mythic land of early America. The "Colonial" style was immediately popular. It was reassuring, confident architecture—something that everyone could relate to.

The Colonial Revival provided a "usable past" for the more recent immigrants as well. From the Centennial in 1876 to the final issue of The Monograph Series in 1940, the foreign-born population of the United States more than doubled. Concerned citizens hoped to turn up the heat on the Great Melting Pot by establishing Colonial Revival settlement houses to help Americanize the immigrants. The famous House of the Seven Gables in Salem, Massachusetts, was first restored in 1909 by Joseph Everett Chandler for use as a settlement house.

The Centennial celebrations provided the spark, and architects went off to gather fuel. Architects Mead, White and Bigelow took a celebrated sketching trip around New England in 1877. In that same year, Charles McKim called for the development of "antiquarian architects, men who are familiar with the history of building, . . . to describe and note whatever they may meet." Rhode Island saw some of the earliest work of the Colonial Revival, such as the Taylor House of Newport, built in 1886 by McKim, Mead, White and Bigelow.

Much of this early work was energetically imaginative, with no more than a nod to historical reality. The details were often greatly exaggerated; with oversized pediments, entablatures and belt courses. It was "modernized Colonial" with its own standards of success. The Ward House built in Lenox, Massachusetts, effectively simulated growth over the years from imitation additions. One enthusiastic critic commented that "but for a few Queen Anne fantasies, it might pass for an old Puritan's homestead."

These symbolic houses had to be furnished with symbolic objects. Every home needed a spinning wheel (emblematic of the "virtue and industry of the past"), flat irons on the hearth, a flintlock over the fireplace, and a grandfather clock in the hall.

Part of the inauthenticity was due to ignorance. No one really knew what the original work looked like—not after a century or two of repairs and improvements. It required decades of field study and the development of inexpensive halftone photograph printing before a more accurate picture could emerge. The *White Pine Series of Architectural Monographs*, begun in 1914, made a lasting contribution (witness the book you have in your hands) to the wider understanding of the historical reality.

But it was only partially ignorance that caused the revival to diverge from the original. The reality of the past may not always meet the needs of the present. In the 1913 book *Colonial Architecture for Those About to Build*, the authors clearly stated their objectives. "It is the desire of every normal person to . . . realize in his surroundings, as far as he may, his ideal." Each generation has felt free to choose that part of the past that met its own ideals. Colonial Revivals should not be confused with attempts at authentic replication of early buildings. The purist can easily scoff, never understanding the creator's intent. The Colonial Revivalist seeks a synthesis, using the evidence of our ancestors as a source for quotation and as a "catalyst to the imagination." Thus we find Colonial homes and gardens flavored with Art Deco or the Moderne.

Now, the aging homes of the Colonial Revival present their own challenge to the preservationist. As our knowledge of the authentic colonial work increases, the temptation is to correct the "inaccuracies." The preservationist, however, must be responsible for both the originals and the revivals. The original may tell us about our ancestors, but the revival tells us about ourselves.

ROY UNDERHILL
MASTER HOUSEWRIGHT
COLONIAL WILLIAMSBURG

Newport,
Rhode Island

Text by
Kenneth Clark
Photographs by
The Author
Originally published in 1922 as White Pine Monograph
Volume VIII, Number 3

DUKE STREET, NEWPORT, RHODE ISLAND
House at Number 5 in the foreground.

NEWPORT: AN EARLY AMERICAN SEAPORT

TO most people Newport means nothing more than the summer playground of the very rich and socially prominent. The mere mention of this Rhode Island wateringplace calls up a conglomerate vision of Society, with a capital "S." Bailey's Beach, the Casino, and The Breakers. While it is true that one part of Newport is occupied by the "show places" which have given the town its reputation for smartness and palatial residences, there is another interest for the architect, that to be found in the old town, full of memories and associations of a former and simpler age.

Newport was once America's foremost seaport, far outstripping New York in volume of shipping and commerce. It boasted a line of vessels sailing direct to London, carrying the sperm oil, candles, woolen goods, and farm produce which the colony exported, as well as the more prosperous citizens as passengers.

The old town lies along the harbor and originally consisted of two streets, Thames Street and Spring Street, paralleling the shoreline and terminating in the parade now known as Washington Square. The town was originally settled by Nicholas Easton and his two sons, who, coming from the Massachusetts Bay Colony, landed May 2, 1639. Other colonists soon joined them, a town was laid out, and a new American commonwealth was begun.

For more than a hundred years the town prospered in peace and plenty, until the mutterings of rebellion were heard, and in 1769, six years before the battle of Lexington, there

occurred here the first act of open rebellion against the mother country. The British ship *Liberty* was seized and scuttled as an act of revenge for outrages perpetrated upon the population by her officers and crew. In 1772 another outbreak occurred, when some townsmen, in retaliation for British oppression, put out in boats and attacked the King's ship *Gaspee*, burned her, and severely wounded her commander. This attack resulted in the first bloodshed in the American war for liberty, and was the first armed resistance to the British navy by the colonies. After the outbreak of the Revolution the sturdy seafarers of the town furnished four thousand men to help man the ships of the new American navy, and from the battle of Lexington to the surrender at Yorktown the men of Newport played a prominent part in all branches of the service. Washington complained that, owing to their hot-headed zeal, the Rhode Island troops gave him more trouble than any others, to which their commander, Colonel Olney, replied, "That is what the enemy says."

In 1776 a British fleet arrived before the town and landed one thousand men, who were quartered in the houses of the citizens. General Prescott was assigned to the command, and he made an imperishable name for himself as a bully and tyrant. His headquarters were the house at the corner of Spring and Pelham streets, which is still standing, unaltered. This unpopular officer was captured during a period of revelry by a detachment of Continentals under Colonel William Barton. The British forces evacuated Newport on October 25, 1779, after a carnival of destruction that left the town almost in ruins. The occupation by the French forces, under the Comte de Rochambeau, occurred shortly after, and they were gladly welcomed by the long-suffering towns-people.

In the narrow, quaint streets of the town along the waterfront there remain many houses of the Revolutionary and pre-Revolutionary period, some sadly in need of repair, and many mutilated beyond restoration. Unfortunately modern Newport does not seem to regard with proper reverence these souvenirs of her greater days, and with a few exceptions

Window Detail

OLD COMMUNITY HOUSE, NEWPORT, RHODE ISLAND

they are fast going to rack and ruin: many of them have been altered for commercial use, and others, fine mansions of a former day, now house foreign laborers, and are little more than tenements.

Many fine houses, however, remain, and few sections of New England can boast of better individual examples. The general impression of architectural type that is gained in the course of a walk about the streets is one of smallness of scale and refinement of detail, essentially domestic in feeling and character. Many of the doorways are rich in a peculiarly naïve ornamental treatment, with Corinthian caps that never graced

WANTON-LYMAN-HAZARD HOUSE, NEWPORT, RHODE ISLAND

OLD BULL MANSION, NEWPORT, RHODE ISLAND

Classic tradition was more accurately followed in Massachusetts, but the craftsmen and designers, though their knowledge of their elements was more manifest, showed no superiority in the actual execution than did those of Newport. There is a certain quality about some of the Newport work that is hard to classify, yet which adds an interest that the more conventional work lacks.

Perhaps the most conventional house in Newport, and one of the best preserved, is the Vernon House, at the corner of Clark and Mary streets. It is in excellent condition and remains as it was in pre-Revolutionary days. It was built in 1758 by one Metcalf Bowler, and in 1773 it came into the possession of William Vernon, a wealthy merchant and ship-owner, and remained in the family until 1872. This

the pages of Vignola or Buhlmann, but are nevertheless beautiful in their expression of the work of the master craftsman of that day, who, perhaps deficient in knowledge of the pure classic detail that the work of the Massachusetts coast boasts, has, however, evolved a somewhat primitive expression of it that abounds in originality and is well worth study.

The architecture of our old coast towns, Newburyport, Salem, Marblehead, Portsmouth, and Newport, all these and others, built and lived in by seafarers, seem to bear the mark of a culture that is not easily accounted for, except as the expression of an innate refinement, broadened by contact with the Old World. In the Massachusetts towns the detail is more refined and seemingly more intimately related to that of the mother country than it is in Newport.

JOHN BANNISTER HOUSE, NEWPORT, RHODE ISLAND

house was occupied by the Comte de Rochambeau during his stay here as commandant of the
allied forces in 1780. During this period many
brilliant fêtes and balls were given by the
Comte in honor of distinguished visitors and
townspeople. Here the victorious General

throughout, and questionable as this treatment
may be for wood, from the standpoint of
theoretical design it seems well excused in this
instance, for the house is a very perfect example
of its kind, and the rustication is carefully
studied in its relation to the openings and to the

Detail of Doorway
JOHN BANNISTER HOUSE (PRESCOTT HEADQUARTERS),
NEWPORT, RHODE ISLAND

Washington was welcomed on March 8, 1782.
The story of eyewitnesses says that he wore the
insignia of a Maréchal of France, and was received with all the pomp and display of a royal
visitation.

The walls of the Vernon House are rusticated

scale of the façades. The details of the front
door and cornice are pure Georgian, well
executed, and the fenestration is particularly
happy. The rear elevation is as interesting as
the front, with its low door under the stair-
landing and the finely proportioned arched

General View of the Rear
VERNON HOUSE (ROCHAMBEAU HEADQUARTERS), NEWPORT, RHODE ISLAND

VERNON HOUSE (ROCHAMBEAU HEADQUARTERS), NEWPORT, RHODE ISLAND

HOUSE AT NUMBER 228 SPRING STREET, NEWPORT, RHODE ISLAND

window, looking out to a space where there was formerly a garden. Though of less magnificent proportions, this house seems well worth ranking with the "great" houses of similar type of Marblehead and Newburyport.

The Wanton-Lyman-Hazard House, at the corner of Broadway and Stone Street, is one of Newport's earliest examples that remains in anything like its original condition. Local tradition dates this house "before 1700," and

Detail of Doorway
NUMBER 27 CHURCH STREET

the primitive framing showing in the interior of the attic story seems to substantiate this claim, as does the coved plaster cornice of the façade, a treatment which is most unusual and of which there are few remaining examples.

Sadly enough, this Newport house is doomed to destruction, for, standing as it does on a very valuable corner lot on Broadway, it will soon have to surrender to commercial necessity and go the way so large

Detail of Doorway
NUMBER 228 SPRING STREET, NEWPORT, RHODE ISLAND

HOUSE AT NUMBER 36 CHURCH STREET, NEWPORT, RHODE ISLAND

Revival, which ran its course with such dire results in the early nineteenth century. The monitor treatment in this example is very well done, and it seems strange that this feature is not used more in modern work, giving as it does a practically full third story without adding to the height of the façade; it would seem to solve the dormer problem in a most satisfactory way.

At 228 Spring Street, on the corner of Leovin Street, there stands a fine type of Newport house. It still retains a front yard which was formerly much larger, but the encroachments of commerce have reduced it to its present dimensions. The elevation facing Spring Street has many fine qualities: the window spacing is excellent and the corner-boards, with their simple, sunk panel, form a fine termination to the horizontal lines of the clapboarding, and add a semblance of strength at the corners that has a

a number of its contemporaries have gone.

The old Bull Mansion, situated at the "First Mile Stone," on Broadway, is a fine foursquare manor house of the 1750 period. Its walls are rusticated, and a beautifully proportioned roof with an embryo monitor break in it has much character. The addition of a porch, of much later date than the house, has ruined the general effect, but an idea can be obtained from the end elevation of its appearance before the porch was added. The roof is odd in that it has both dormers and a monitor break in which there are no windows. Judging from its detail the roof construction is of the same date as the main house.

There are several houses here with full monitor roofs, of the typical Rhode Island type so familiar in Providence and Bristol. The house at 115 Pelham Street is one of the best of these, but of a later date, and shows in the details the beginnings of the influence of the Greek

HOUSE AT NUMBER 27 CHURCH STREET, NEWPORT, RHODE ISLAND

NUMBER 5 DUKE STREET

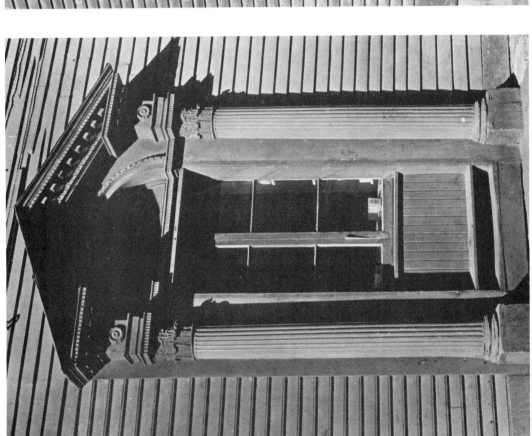

MASON HOUSE

TWO DOORWAYS IN NEWPORT, RHODE ISLAND

ST. JOSEPH'S SCHOOL

NUMBER 119 SPRING STREET

TWO DOORWAYS IN NEWPORT, RHODE ISLAND

Detail of Doorway
HOUSE AT NUMBER 228 SPRING STREET, NEWPORT, RHODE ISLAND

satisfying effect. The entrance is most interesting; a decided originality shows in the use and
execution of the details. The pediment, slightly
too low for ideal proportions, is embellished with
rosettes and modillions on its soffit, and the pecu-
liar abacus of the Corinthian cap, with its flowing curves in plan, is unique. It will be noted that
the mouldings of the abacus carry across the door
lintel and form a tie between the two columns,
which otherwise would look rather loose and un-
connected. The clapboarding is uniformly spaced
through the whole height of the façade and its
edge is moulded. There are evidently two levels

the faces of the modillions bear a panel with a
rosette. The soffit has a strap ornament of in-
terlaced pattern, instead of rosettes, which looks
more finished. The house itself is well proportioned with a simple ridge roof. An interesting
detail is the method by which the cornice has
been made and its relation to the upper part of
the corner-board, and the mouldings over the
second-story window heads.

The John Bannister House (now called The
Prescott, because it was once the headquarters
of General Prescott), at the corner of Pelham
and Spring streets, has a gambrel roof of rather

WHITEHORSE TAVERN, NEWPORT, RHODE ISLAND

on the ground floor, for the windows of the side
street elevation are stepped up with the grade of
the street, which is considerable.

It is interesting to compare the doorway of the
house at 228 Spring Street with that of the house
at 27 Church Street, which is somewhat similar
in general design but totally different in detail.
The capitals in the latter are of Doric-Corinthian
combination that has almost the character of
an Adam detail, and the proportion of the entablature and its component parts is much better, more refined, and in accordance with accepted proportions: but even here the originality
of the craftsman has made itself evident, for the
fascia of the cornice has been denticulated and

fine proportions, with three well designed dormers. The recessed entrance motive is a feature
rare in Newport, and its treatment here with
colonnettes and elliptically arched head is well
thought out. The mouldings of the cornice supporting the soffit are beautifully profiled, and
form an interesting contrast to the stubby crown
moulding with its narrow fascia just above it.

At 5 Duke Street is a fine doorway with excellent detail; brackets, beautifully designed,
supporting a pedimented doorhead. This is
the only example of this type in Newport, and
seems to bear the mark of a more sophisticated
hand than the average work.

There are other examples in Newport worthy

of detailed description, but to do this would unduly prolong the text, and is unnecessary, for many of them are illustrated herein.

The old houses of Newport, because of their location in the heart of the business section, are being menaced; in all probability they will soon be torn down or unrecognizably altered. Architecturally speaking, old Newport is too little known, and this photographic record of its early achievement should be a valuable contribution to the history of early American domestic architecture.

Bristol, Rhode Island
Part One

Text by
William J. Burleigh
Photographs by
Arthur C. Haskell

Originally published in 1936 as White Pine Monograph
Volume XXII, Number 3

NUMBER 86 STATE STREET, BRISTOL, RHODE ISLAND

THE HOUSES OF BRISTOL, RHODE ISLAND, PART ONE

BRISTOL is one of the principal settlements made along the eastern shore of Narragansett Bay. Intended in the first instance as the harbor or most important seaport of Plymouth Colony, it was planned upon a far more liberal scale than any other settlement that had been made in New England up to that time.

The Grand Articles, in which the arrangement and requirements of the town and its buildings were set forth, was a rather unusual document for that period and time. Not only did it specify the plan of the town, with its three principal streets—Thames, Hope and High streets—running parallel with the waterfront, of established widths—to be crossed by other streets at right angles, also of specified widths and lengths; but it was further required that "all houses should be two stories high, with not less than two good rooms on a floor." There were eighteen signers to these original articles, and the town layout provided for 128 house lots. These same articles stated in no uncertain terms that the town was being established "for purposes of trade and commerce!"

At an early time this entire peninsula was known as the Mount Hope Lands, which some writers claim to have been derived from the Indian name of Montaup. At the time of the settlement of the adjoining colonies to the north and east, these lands were in the possession of the tribes ruled by Massasoit, the friend of the settlers; and he is claimed to have had one residence established upon the slopes of this same mountain. King Philip, a third generation descendant from Massasoit, was wounded and killed in a swamp near the base of Mount Hope, on August 12, 1676.

All the land along this shore of the bay was awarded to Plymouth Colony by a special grant of the King, Charles II, signed January 12, 1680. The 7,000 acres of this land, including Mount Hope Neck and Poppasquash Neck, were in turn sold for £1100 on September 14, 1680, to four well known residents of Boston, John Walley, Nathaniel Byfield, Stephen Burton and Nathaniel Oliver, who were among the original signers of the articles.

It is believed the name was taken from the seaport of Bristol, on the west coast of England, as it was intended that the new settlement should rival that busy harbor in its maritime importance—and it seems to have been, from an early date, an important shipping town vying with the settlements of Providence, Newport and Warren, in its coastal and shipping business. By 1690 it had fifteen vessels engaged in foreign commerce. In 1686 a large shipment of fine horses was made to Surinam in Dutch Guiana; but the principal trade of the vessels outfitted here, as well as the other settlements mentioned, was in rum, slaves and molasses!

By that time, and for many years thereafter, the best established and most profitable voyages were made upon the simple plan of sailing the first leg of the voyage to Africa, with hogsheads of rum and trinkets destined to appeal to the natives. Along the African coast, the skippers would anchor until they were able to exchange this cargo for blacks, when they would set out upon the middle passage to the West Indies, where the slaves were in turn exchanged for casks of molasses — and the third stage of the voyage was the run back to the home port, where the molasses was distilled into rum; and the ships would be reprovisioned and sail off upon their triangular ventures again.

That this was a very profitable trade the many large established fortunes of the various New England seaports prove most certainly. At one time there were five distilleries in Bristol, while the value of its trade with Africa, the West Indies and the Spanish Main, made its wharves busy with men and covered with

further to the north; a three-story-front-lean-to type, with an end overhang at the third-floor level. This building contains two exceptionally interesting rooms. To some they will be interesting because of their historical associations, as Lafayette occupied the northeast room upon the second floor during September of 1778, while the French regiments engaged in the blockade of Newport were encamped upon Bradford Hill nearby. The woodwork in this room, as well as all that in the room directly under it upon the first floor, still displays its early "marbleized"

PARKER-BORDEN HOUSE, 736 HOPE STREET, BRISTOL, RHODE ISLAND

warehouses from the early years of its settlement. By 1774 it had a population of 1209, of whom 114 were blacks. This had increased to over 1600 by the end of the century and to fully 3000 by 1820.

The oldest house, known as the Bosworth House, is still standing just north of the bridge entering the town, but it has been so changed by interior alteration, additions of various later wings and, finally, a porch with Greek columns, that its original age would hardly now be suspected.

More interesting is the Joseph Reynolds House, still

painting, which has been upon these rooms since the earliest records that have been found. An endeavor to suggest this treatment has been attempted in the measured drawings shown in this chapter. Both the rooms are so dark in color, and so crowded, that it was difficult to secure satisfactory photographic records. The room upon the first floor is now in use as the library of the present owner, and all the new shelving has been carefully painted to match the old work. The old fireplace, unfortunately, became unsafe, and was removed years ago; a new one on the first floor having been

Mantel
PARKER-BORDEN HOUSE, BRISTOL, RHODE ISLAND

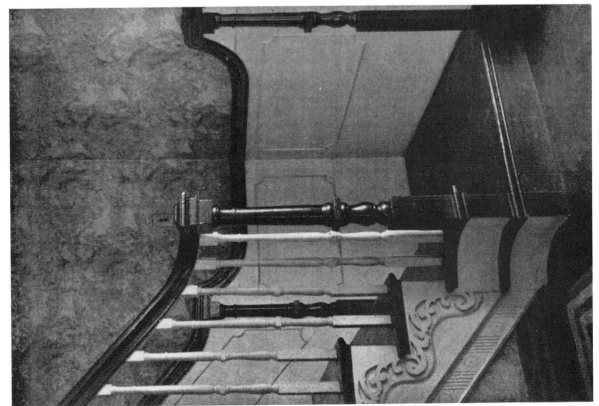

NUMBER 707 HOPE STREET

PARKER-BORDEN HOUSE

TWO EXAMPLES OF OLD STAIRCASES, BRISTOL, RHODE ISLAND

HOUSE AT NUMBER 86 STATE STREET, BRISTOL, RHODE ISLAND

built with a smaller flue to carry through the roof.

These two rooms possess similar details, and mantels, as unusual as any in New England; being of a scale and type that strongly suggest their Elizabethan counterparts in England—a derivation that is even more directly evident in the sturdy oak balusters and rail details of the staircase. The painted treatment of the woodwork in these two rooms recalls the painted woodwork in the room from Marmion, now to be seen in the Metropolitan Museum in New York.

Bristol men and boats also took part in that other

house of Deputy-Governor Bradford, the finest residence in town, located on the Mount—which was rebuilt and where Washington was entertained on the occasion of his visit in 1793. One further relic of the Revolution may be found in the old gambrel-roofed Barracks, a small house, originally built for the troops on Poppasquash Neck, during the war, and then removed across the harbor on the ice during the winter of 1779–1780. It may be seen on the west side of High Street, just north of Bradford.

The land upon which Bristol is built was originally

HOUSE AT NUMBER 67 CHURCH STREET, BRISTOL, RHODE ISLAND

well known local Revolutionary episode, already mentioned in connection with the history of the John Brown House (Volume VI, Chapter 14)—as a whale boat from Bristol, manned by Bristol mariners under command of Captain Simeon Potter, rowed up the bay to take part in the attack upon the *Gaspee*, on the night of June 10, 1772.

On October 7, 1775, Bristol was bombarded by the British fleet; and again attacked on Sunday, May 5, 1778, when they burned the center of the town, as well as some of the outlying mansions, including the

Massachusetts. During its first seventy years, it belonged in turn to the Plymouth, Massachusetts Bay and Rhode Island colonies—coming into the possession of the latter by 1746–1747!

The majority of its beautiful residences are to be found along Hope and High streets, which parallel Thames Street, along the waterfront. While the beautiful doorways for which this town is famous have been retained in most instances, along with certain curious details of windows and cornices (of which the example chosen for the frontispiece is one of the most

Hall
NUMBER 67 CHURCH STREET, BRISTOL, RHODE ISLAND

DEWOLF HOUSE, 132 HIGH STREET

NUMBER 67 CHURCH STREET

TWO EXAMPLES OF THE OLD STAIRCASES IN BRISTOL, RHODE ISLAND

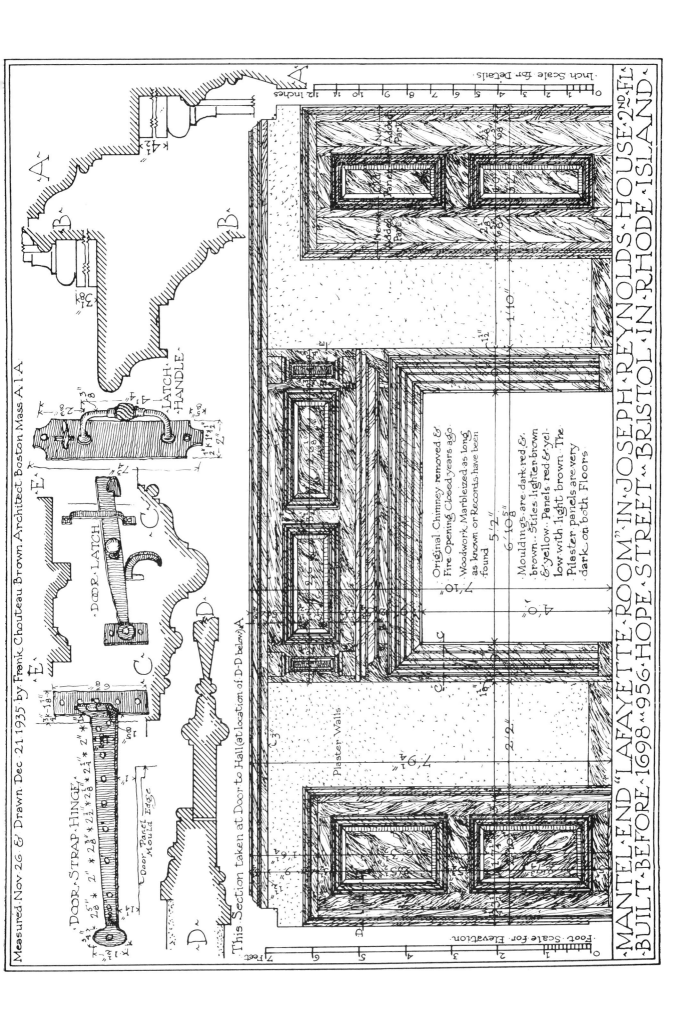

JOSEPH REYNOLDS HOUSE—1698—NUMBER 956 HOPE STREET, BRISTOL, RHODE ISLAND

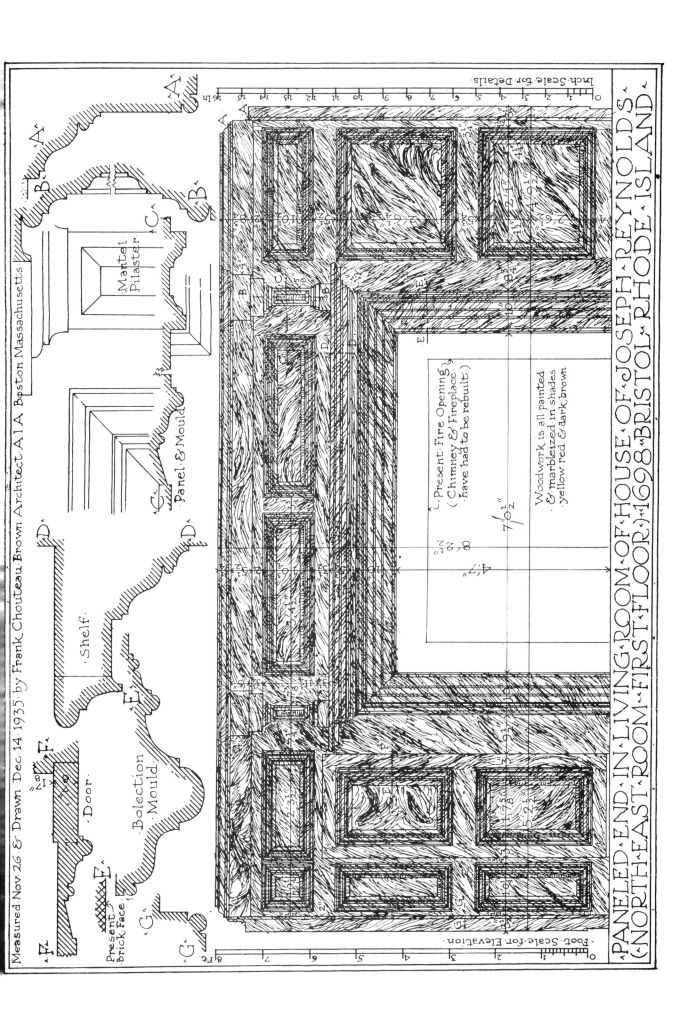

Measured Nov. 26 & Drawn Dec. 14. 1935. by Frank Chouteau Brown. Architect. A I A. Boston Massachusetts.

Mantel Pilaster.

Panel & Mould.

Shelf.

Bolection Mould.

Door.

Present Brick Face.

Inch Scale for Details

Foot Scale for Elevation

(Present Fire Opening . Chimney & Fireplace . have had to be rebuilt.)

Woodwork is all painted & marbleized in shades . yellow red & dark brown.

.PANELED.END.IN.LIVING.ROOM.OF.HOUSE.OF.JOSEPH.REYNOLDS.
.(NORTHEAST.ROOM.FIRST.FLOOR.).1698.BRISTOL.RHODE.ISLAND.

Staircase
CAPT. LITTLEFIELD HOUSE, BRISTOL, RHODE ISLAND

curious! Another unusual detail found on this same structure is that the corners have been ornamented with quoins, but placed *diagonally*, instead of horizontally!). A great many of the dwellings have been so "improved" internally, that it is very hard now to find original interior woodwork in the rooms of the more important houses.

Many of the old staircases remain, both the sturdy early Tudor type found in the Reynolds House, and the extremely delicate, dainty details such as appear in the Dr. DeWolf House on High Street! Among the many examples of stair rails and balusters, the utmost ingenuity seems to have been expended on the cutting of the string faces, and treatment of the newels.

Only four miles south of Warren, it is not to be unexpected that many of the mantel treatments, dadoes, and moulding details found, are often similar to the examples that already have been shown from that adjoining township. This similarity may be easily traced in one or two of the examples from Bristol that are illustrated. Here, even more than in the neighbor town, are found elaborate treatments of the wall side of the staircase runs—dadoes, elaborately ramped and paneled; or with half balusters against the wallboard repeating the open side of the stair; or fluted pilasters or half-turned posts, repeating the landing or newel posts, and often of mahogany, as well!

Indeed, many of the doorways, moulding sections, and staircase details to be seen in Bristol—as well as at Warren—may be found duplicated in the larger and more imposing residences upon College Hill in Providence, or the older streets of other portions of that city and its suburbs. For it is about the shores of Narragansett Bay, a body of water thirty miles long and 250 square miles in area, of about one-fifth the total area of the entire state, that the best architecture surviving from the colonial and earlier periods of the Providence Plantations is still to be found!

Mantel

NUMBER II CHURCH STREET, BRISTOL, RHODE ISLAND

Staircase
MERRIMAN HOUSE, BRISTOL, RHODE ISLAND

Bristol, Rhode Island
Part Two

Text by
William J. Burleigh
Photographs by
Arthur C. Haskell
Originally published in 1936 as White Pine Monograph
Volume XXII, Number 4

NUMBER II CHURCH STREET, BRISTOL, RHODE ISLAND

THE HOUSES OF BRISTOL, RHODE ISLAND, PART TWO

ALTHOUGH the several depredations made by the British during the Revolutionary War resulted in the destruction of many of Bristol's houses — and especially the foray of May 5, 1778, when the Hessians burnt all the buildings in the center of the town, so that many of the early dwellings that once stood along its well ordered street plan disappeared in 1780 — that same factor has left the township today presenting an unusually consistent and harmonious picture to the modern visitor. This leaves the greater majority of its older structures dating from between 1780 and 1820, and most of these belong to the last half of this forty-year period, while a few important structures would even appear as being better dated within a few following years. This stricture would even be largely true of the DeWolf-Colt Mansion which — although built in 1810 — has actually been altered into the appearance of a near-Victorian dwelling as it is now to be seen, surrounded by an unusual example of early American wrought iron fence, with two single side and one central double gateway, the character of which may be studied in both the photographs and measured drawings included in this chapter.

In addition to this house, which is among the most pretentious of the dwellings now to be found along Bristol's principal thoroughfare, several others remain that, in their present state, represent very nearly the same period — even though most of them are actually of an earlier date. However, these later dwellings, mainly from the hand of Mr. Russell Warren, a local architect whose work has previously been well documented, have already been pretty well presented — at least so far as their exteriors are concerned and so it is hardly pertinent again to dwell at this time upon their several individual and excellent traits.

It might be said that their interiors, so far as they still exhibit woodwork of the original period, are generally extremely simple. The staircases, while delicate and tasteful in design, usually have small square balusters — seven-eighths inch square, or less — a delicately turned newel; or their slight mahogany railing is wound up into a beautifully proportioned starting scroll. The gallery board and stair ends are also extremely simple, with a few light mouldings — or a simply outlined bracket, or double curved connecting scroll, of slight relief, as their principal outstanding expressions of design.

The other elements of their interior finish are equally restrained; with door and window architraves of the delicately moulded type associated with the early 1800's, and doors with six or eight lightly sunk and frequently inner moulded panels, often with a raised center, or with an applied reed inner moulding emphasizing the proportions of the panel outlines. Many of the original wooden mantels have been removed in favor of the more imposing marble substitutes that became fashionable a generation or less after; for most of these houses have suffered — along with almost all the interiors of the town — from its several eras of prosperity; during which these dwellings were so generally "renovated" or "modernized" that their original charms have often become somewhat tainted by the bolder detail and more cumbersome weight of the woodwork of the Greek Revival, along with the still later — and even more questionable — taste of the early Victorian period!

It is from some such "sea-change" as these, that the present DeWolf-Colt Mansion, originally built in 1810, now presents a rather overpowering picture of the 1850's! And along with many another handsome Bristol dwelling it has lost its original charm in the process of being "brought up to date" — with the inten-

House — generally more widely known as the House with the Eagles — which also remains well preserved to intrigue the visitor in the center of the town, upon the western side of Hope Street. Another example of Mr. Russell Warren's work; it was built in 1807, and one of its owners was that Capt. Churchill, who commanded the famous privateer *Yankee*; which was outfitted and sailed from Bristol on the first of six successful voyages, immediately the War of 1812 broke out. In less than three months she had made ten prizes, and in three years her captures had been valued at £1,000,000! While the exterior of this house remains

NUMBER 21 BRADFORD STREET, BRISTOL, RHODE ISLAND

tion of making it more "modern" or "convenient" — by its owner in some subsequent period of prosperity.

Such is not the case, however, with the two notable examples that must at least be mentioned, although for various reasons they do not appear illustrated here. One is the well known DeWolf-Middleton House ("Hey-Bonnie Hall") that is still preserved and to be seen on Poppasquash Neck. It continues to present a rare and delightful picture of the northern house with southern plan, reproducing in its new habitat the characteristic and generous "wings" of the old Virginia plantation house. The other is the Cabot-Churchill

unspoiled, and is one of the most familiar and well known designs in the town (see Volume I, Chapter 5), the interior — also little changed — is among the simplest and perhaps least "architectural" products from Mr. Warren's pencil.

The previous chapter showed the Joseph Reynolds House, and mentioned the old Bosworth House, of about the same date (1680), but now much changed. It did not illustrate the house of Deputy-Governor Bradford, on the Mount, originally one of the finest houses in the town, which was rebuilt immediately after the second British raid, in 1778. Another De-

Doorway Detail
NUMBER 11 CHURCH STREET, BRISTOL, RHODE ISLAND

Wolf house, setting well back from the roadway, in an old plantation of trees, may be seen partway from the town to the Mount. It is sometimes called the DeWolf Farmhouse—and besides its usual types of local interiors also contains one curious room with heavy Elizabethan woodwork, so dark in tone that it could not be rendered with justice by the camera. A word might be said in addition about the house to the west of 86 State Street, which, besides some original mantels, has a curious treatment of the corner posts in one of its rooms. As used there, the plaster walls of

cases, particularly of the 1780–1820 period, that still exist in this town; perhaps its most noted characteristic for the traveler—who is unable to penetrate sufficiently into the interiors of these dwellings to realize the variety of old staircases they still contain—is to be found in the many fine doorways with which Bristol seems particularly to abound.

A few of the most individual of these doorways are reproduced. Perhaps the most decorative and unusual type of them all is to be seen in its finest manifestations at Warren (Vol. VI, Chap. 4). It is the doorway with

NUMBER 149 HIGH STREET, BRISTOL, RHODE ISLAND

the room continue without break into the internal corner angle, and then the "post" is placed—entirely clear of the walls—*inside* that angle, as a round post or unmoulded column, extending from floor to ceiling!

Another unusual structure is the old Poor House, built by Capt. James DeWolf; a commodious and sturdy structure of masonry, now plastered over, only a short distance from Hope Street, along one of the roads leading to Poppasquash Neck from near the location of the Joseph Reynolds House.

Aside from the many excellent examples of stair-

circular toplight, often with carved muntins, enclosed within an open pediment, of variously designed mouldings (but all ornate and richly carved), and the finest of them are also usually given a finely carved eagle at the pediment peak or crossbar center, one or two even having two other birds added at the start of the pediment cornice slope.

One of the most unusual architectural features to be seen in Bristol is the ironwork now in front of the De-Wolf-Colt Mansion. While there still are to be found many examples of the skill of early blacksmiths, in al-

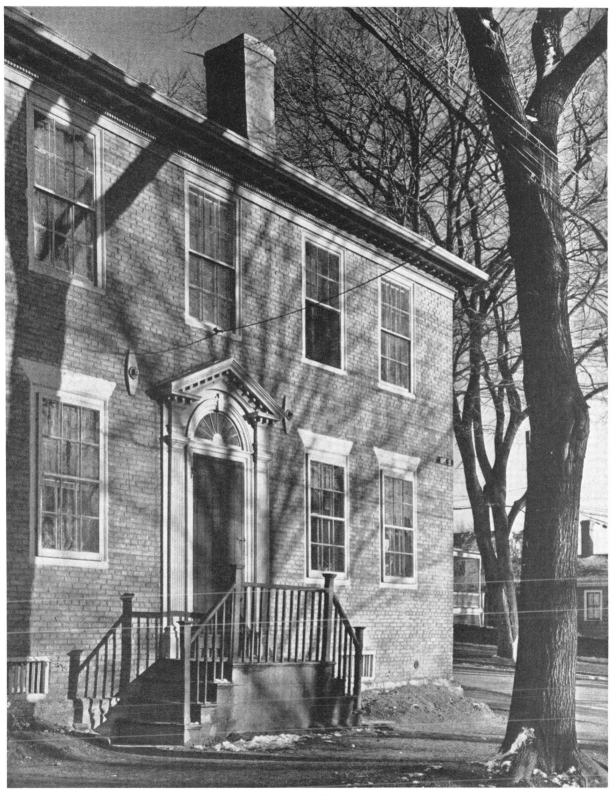

Doorway and Corner
HOPE AND UNION STREETS, BRISTOL, RHODE ISLAND

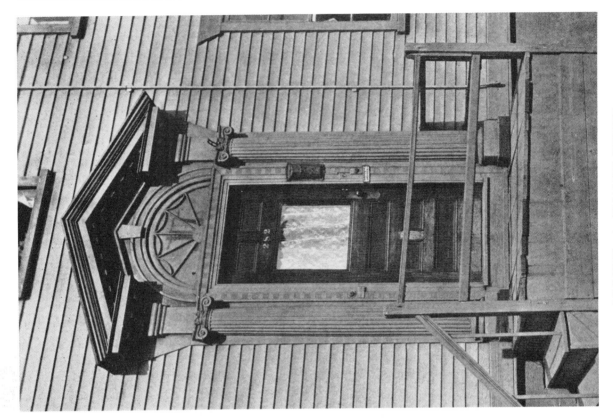

NUMBER 282 THAMES STREET

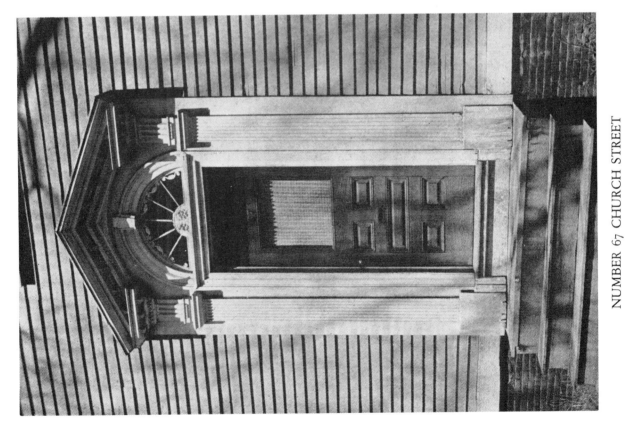

NUMBER 67 CHURCH STREET

OLD DOORWAYS IN BRISTOL, RHODE ISLAND

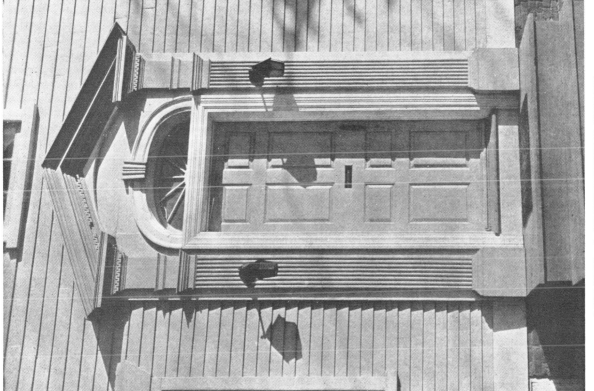

NUMBER 290 HOPE STREET

NUMBER 28 CONSTITUTION STREET

OLD DOORWAYS IN BRISTOL, RHODE ISLAND

most every section of this country where examples of other early crafts originated; most of such work has come down to us in the form of accessory metal hardware required on the old buildings of the vicinity; or such fireirons and utensils as were used about the fireplace and kitchen hearth—particularly many beautifully wrought pieces of iron cooking utensils or lighting equipment devised by these early metal craftsmen to meet the needs or suit the requirements of early settlers.

In certain sections, too, there remain many beautiful examples of iron balustrades or step railings—as in Bowers House in Somerset, Massachusetts. While this unusual dwelling was built in 1770, it was further embellished and beautified in about 1820; at or about which time it may well have been that this graceful and charmingly designed fence railing was also added.

While its skill of craftsmanship may almost be considered as dateless, its flowing graces of line and curve can hardly have developed at as early a time as the building of the old house fronting out upon the river at Somerset. It is, indeed, more than probable that the present roadway, passing along the waterfront between

MORIA-BABBIT HOUSE—c1810—NUMBER 328 HOPE STREET, BRISTOL, RHODE ISLAND

Maryland, northern New York State, or Louisiana—along with a few sections of street or yard fencing. But it is rare, indeed, to find in northeastern New England, an instance of wrought iron enclosing grille so considerable in extent and fine and delicate in design as now extends along the very considerable frontage of this mansion upon Hope Street in Bristol.

There persists a legend that this fence was not the product of a local smithy, but that the original gates and sections of the fence were brought years ago from in front of an even earlier mansion, the Jerathmael

the handsome row of old dwellings that still distinguish this small town from most of its neighbors, was not originally in existence—and that the lawns of all these dwellings—along with their gardens—then extended uninterruptedly down to the water's edge.

But the brownstone terrace wall and coping that still mark the present street line of this old dwelling, also show the lead-filled cuttings into which the individual iron bars of a fence of exactly this design might have been set—and to that extent, at least, this legend may seem to be substantiated.

GOVERNOR BRADFORD HOUSE, BRISTOL, RHODE ISLAND

WROUGHT IRON GATE—COLT MANSION, BRISTOL, RHODE ISLAND

Measured June 10 & Drawn July 5 1936. by Frank Chouteau Brown Architect Boston Massachusetts.

·A·I·A·

South Terminal of Fence.

Detail of Rosette & Scroll

·N·B· This Ironwork is supposed to have been taken from the Jerathmael Bowers House in Somerset Massachusetts. Its probable date should be about 1815~1825.

Top Finial.

Center Stop & Support Double Gate

½ Inch Scale for Details
Foot Scale for Elevation

Wall of Brownstone in Blocks 5'5" long by 1'0" thick

·WROUGHT·IRON·FENCE·&·GATEWAYS· ·DEWITT·COLT·MANSION· ·REMOVED·FROM·BOWERS·HOUSE·SOMERSET·(MAS)·TO·BRISTOL·RHODE·ISLAND·

Measured June 10 1936 & Drawn June 24 1936 by   Frank Chouteau Brown Architect Boston Mass.

4 Ft

Foot Scale for Elevation.

1'·5"

11½"

¼"×1"

½"×1¼"

4'·1"

Red
Gl·Purple

Eng·
Glass
Red

White

Hexagonal
Lantern.

2'·½"

¼"×1"

8'·3"

6'·4"

4'·4"

2'·3"

44¼"   44¼"

Inch. Scale for Details.

1⅞"×1¼"

1⅜×½"

⅞"×1"

1'·5¼"

⅞"×1"

½"×1"

⅝"×1"

½"×1"

CENTRE·DOUBLE·GATEWAY·DeWITT·COLT·MANSION·
·ON·HOPE·STREET·AT·BRISTOL·IN·RHODE·ISLAND·

Iron Gate
COLT MANSION, BRISTOL, RHODE ISLAND

NUMBER 1061 HOPE STREET, BRISTOL, RHODE ISLAND

NUMBER 75 CONSTITUTION STREET, BRISTOL, RHODE ISLAND

NUMBER 34 OLIVER STREET, BRISTOL, RHODE ISLAND

Doorway Detail
NUMBER 154 HIGH STREET, BRISTOL, RHODE ISLAND

Warren, Rhode Island
Part One

Text by
J. Fenimore Russell
Photographs by
Arthur C. Haskell
Originally published in 1935 as White Pine Monograph
Volume XXI, Number 5

MONROE HOUSE, 116 CHILD STREET, WARREN, RHODE ISLAND

SOME OLD HOUSES OF WARREN, RHODE ISLAND, PART ONE

IN the light of present day tolerance, the first founders and settlers of the Massachusetts Bay colonies appear to have been unduly severe and bigoted in their requirements for admission to communal fellowship. No individual was allowed a vote in the temporal affairs of the community unless he had first been accepted as a full member of the Church organization. In that entire area there was no distinction made between Church and State; but the two were fused together, and so continued for many years.

Possibly it might be claimed that the various settlements were all experiments toward achieving a Christian commonwealth; in which the individuals controlling the social and economic direction of the group were dominated by a common community of spiritual belief. Even those dissenting on what may appear to us today to be the most trivial points of the theology established in these new settlements, were severely treated by the community; not permitted any voice in the temporal affairs of the colony; and often banished or transported from within the limits of its jurisdiction.

This explains the considerable number of dissenters, who left Massachusetts Bay or Plymouth, either singly or in groups, during the early years of the history of that region. It was also to be expected that the substitution of a new system of land ownership — the transmitting of property by inheritance, instead of the Old World feudal system of land control — must have gradually worked toward a wider and more democratic distribution and holding of land.

Within the area of Rhode Island, and the Providence Plantations, however, a spirit of wider tolerance was established and maintained from the very first years of the settlement of its earliest colonies. This tolerance was further upheld by the class of settlers who traced their way through the dense wilderness separating Boston and Plymouth from Narragansett Bay, in order to express their disagreement with the beliefs or practices upheld by the strict churchmen and their congregations along the shores of Massachusetts Bay.

Among the earliest and best known of these were Roger Williams, William Blackstone, and Anne Hutchinson. Mistress Hutchinson believed that people were saved by their "faith," while the General Court of Massachusetts — upheld by the rigid religious tenets that permeated the church members of which it was composed — declared that people could only be saved "by their works."

Of course Roger Williams was perhaps the first of these remonstrants to remove himself from the dictates and control of the Massachusetts colonies. And after he had first established himself on a site that he believed to be outside that province, a year later he again removed to the other bank of the Blackstone River, in order to avoid any possible doubt as he had found that Plymouth Colony had made certain claims to the region to the north and east of this same narrow waterway.

Thus, while the Massachusetts Bay and Plymouth colonies had been founded in the first place by dissenters from the beliefs of the Church of England, in search of a land where they could find freedom of religious thought and liberty in its expression — yet they had so little consideration for those others who happened not to think exactly as they did themselves, that the records of the early years immediately succeeding the establishment of these settlements are filled with the names of individuals and groups who—not content with the limited "freedom" they found there in this New World—were inspired to move elsewhere.

So it was that, in 1638, John Clarke and William Coddington, with Anne's husband William Hutchinson and a few others, set sail for Delaware; but the roughness of the ocean off Cape Cod caused them to land and travel overland to Providence, where Roger Williams secured for them from the Aquidneck Indians the island then called Rhode Island, and so the second settlement was made in Portsmouth, on what is now known as Newport Island. A year later Anne Hutchinson came, and shortly after—in that same year—Clarke and Coddington and eleven others, disagreeing with the Hutchinsons, moved further along the island, and so Newport itself came to be the third settlement established in that region.

Then Warwick on Greenwich Bay became the fourth, when in 1643 Samuel Cotton and eleven other Providence families settled there. The fifth was Westerly, founded in 1661 and incorporated in 1670; while New Shoreham (Block Island) was settled in the same year. North Kingston was settled in 1641 and incorporated 1674, and Conanicut Island (Jamestown) was settled in 1657 and incorporated in 1678.

As the land where the town of Warren now lies was not at that time a part of Rhode Island, its name does not appear in the list of early settlements named above. The whole matter was so confusing and long-drawn-out a process that it would seem best to reserve its explanation to another place. Suffice it for the moment to state that a portion of its present area was purchased from the Indians in 1644, when the Rev. Samuel Newman, with part of his congregation, removed from Weymouth to take up house lots along this eastern side of Narragansett Bay; at the confluence of two peaceful landlocked bodies of water—now known as the Barrington and Warren Rivers.

The land was greatly fertile; the surrounding waterways abounded in fish and shellfish. The selected site provided ample and protected harborage, near a considerable body of open water upon which other settlements were being established opening easily out into the ocean a bare twenty miles to the south.

Yet the growth of this community seems to have been comparatively slow. By 1746—nearly one hundred years later—the population of Warren was recorded as being only 4767; of whom 4196 were whites, 343 blacks, and 228 were of Indian blood. By 1711 shipbuilding had become an important industry in this region. In Westerly ships had been built since 1681. In Portsmouth and Newport, on Newport Island; and in Providence at the head of the bay, the industry was flourishing. Other shipyards were estab-

lished at Bristol next door where it continues down to the present day. Undoubtedly, much of the delicacy and individuality of the interior woodwork still to be found about this region derives from the skill of these early craftsmen in shipbuilding—just as the especial beauty of the carving shown about the over-light in many a Warren doorway came from the dexterity acquired in the handling of wood by others who had had their training in this same thorough craft of shipbuilding.

The town plan is of the simplest and most natural arrangement possible. Most of the old houses are to be found upon the two principal streets, running almost exactly parallel and north and south, and named obviously enough as Water and Main streets; and the half-dozen short connecting streets that run at right angles in between. At one end, these east and west streets usually continue down to the water front, which lies directly back of the houses along the western side of Water Street, and connect with some old pier, dock, shipyard, or storage sheds; while the greater majority of them stop against Main Street, on their eastern end. The fact of the matter is that both Warren (and Bristol, directly to its south) are built along a narrow peninsula between these two bodies of water, which is separated from Newport Island (still further to the south) by a wide and deep channel.

Most of the dwellings characteristic of Warren are of three—or possibly four—types. The region still contains a number of story-and-a-half cottages, some with gambrel roofs, remaining from its earlier period. Besides these there are to be found a considerable number of simple yet capaciously comfortable dwellings, with four windows spaced across the front of the second story, and the entrance doorway set off the center of the front, under one of the two central openings. An excellent example of this sort of front may be found on page 64, in the house at 211 Water Street. This house also shows the uneven fenestration of the end elevation on the narrower half of the front, that is often found as a part of this arrangement. Sometimes the narrow corner space is a small room; sometimes part of a rather spacious stair hall. The other example, which may be found in the house from 582 Main Street, on page 68, had originally the same fenestration upon the street front (although in this instance accompanied by an even spacing of the end windows upon the wider end). The end extension—in the nature of a bay added to the further end of the dwelling—was a later addition, made at some time in order to enlarge the small room in this house at the right of the entrance doorway.

Houses of a little later period were usually built after the more conventional arrangement of the central doorway with two windows spaced upon each side. The older examples of this class are usually those

SYDNEY DEAN HOUSE, GREEN STREET, WARREN, RHODE ISLAND

HOUSE AT NUMBER 211 WATER STREET, WARREN, RHODE ISLAND

having the old type of gambrel roof so consistently found throughout the entire state of Rhode Island. An example typical of this group may be seen at the foot of page 65. Finally, there are the more nearly square houses—dating usually in this locality from about the turn of the century—of which the house on the corner of Water and Washington streets, placed on page 73, may serve as sufficient illustration.

The town and its environs also boasts of a few examples of brick dwelling architecture, one or two of which appear to suggest that they may have been veneered over an earlier wooden house design. One of these brick dwellings is the simple but well-proportioned Monroe House, reproduced on page 60, built by a mason for his own use about 1820. This house now possesses a most glorious blend of color from the mellowing of the old bricks under the influence of sunlight and weather. Unfortunately most of the other brick dwellings in the town have been coated heavily with paint, so that they now do not possess this particular charm.

But most of the important dwellings of the town show what seems to be the more favorite gable end treatment that, in some of the later and more elaborate examples, such as the Sydney Dean House, formerly located on Main Street, but now removed to an inconspicuous location near the easterly end of Green Street, provides an opportunity to carry the full cornice from the main frontage of the structure up along the rake of the end gable, with all the elaborateness of dentiling or bracketing that has been established for the principal elevation. The same treatment is consistently maintained for the sloping cornices of the door pediments over the inevitable semicircular toplights, to which about all the more elaborately designed doorways conform.

Of this type the two best examples are those shown from 582 Main Street (page 67) and the two doorways on page 74—of which the one with the carved eagle, from 395 Water Street, is probably the most beautiful example now to be found in the town.

Another unusual example, of fine simplicity and

proportions, and undoubtedly earlier date, is the double-width doorway from 25 Washington Street (page 66). All these examples show the favorite local treatment of the addition of a pair of blind doors, hung on heavily offset hinges, so that on a hot summer day, these outer blind doors may be closed and bolted and the solid inner door left open to allow the breeze from the bayside to draw through the central hallway.

The illustrations contained within this chapter display two of the most interesting and characteristic of the mantels now to be found in the Warren town houses. With the single exception of the Waterman House mantel (which may be seen also on page 76) they are the most elaborate of those now remaining in *situ*. Exception may be taken to their characteristic proportions. All show a rather high shelf, with an unusual height of frieze over the fire opening, and a correspondingly short pilaster bounding the wide panel of the overmantel. While these rooms are all of comfortable height — about nine feet in the clear — in order to provide room for the desired treatment of the mantel top,

the upper mantel cornice has to be kept well below the bottom of the room cornice above, with the attending somewhat awkward and stunted effect that may be noted upon these upper plasters.

While most of the mouldings used in these mantelpieces are ornamented; the ornamenting is of the simplest handcut type; and usually of a nature that could be produced by the use of about a quarter-inch half-round gouge chisel; as may be seen by referring to the measured drawings. These mantel designs are also remarkable for the very small — not to say minute — size of some of the mouldings employed; many being of only one-eighth and three-sixteenths inch dimension; a matter that has made these drawings appear both more crowded and "busier" than the mantels actually appear in reality. It should be noted also that the interest of the wood treatment is not confined solely to the mantel, but is carried with equal consistency entirely around the rooms; along the dado and cornice — about the doorways and windows, and even upon the decorative treatment of the cased corner posts!

HOUSE AT NUMBER 25 WASHINGTON STREET, WARREN, RHODE ISLAND

NUMBER 211 WATER STREET

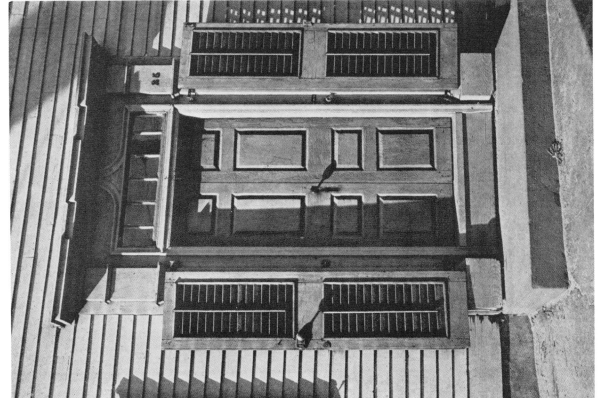

NUMBER 25 WASHINGTON STREET

DOORWAYS IN WARREN, RHODE ISLAND

NUMBER 41 STATE STREET

NUMBER 582 MAIN STREET

DOORWAYS IN WARREN, RHODE ISLAND

HOUSE AT NUMBER 125 WATER STREET, WARREN, RHODE ISLAND

HOUSE AT NUMBER 582 MAIN STREET, WARREN, RHODE ISLAND

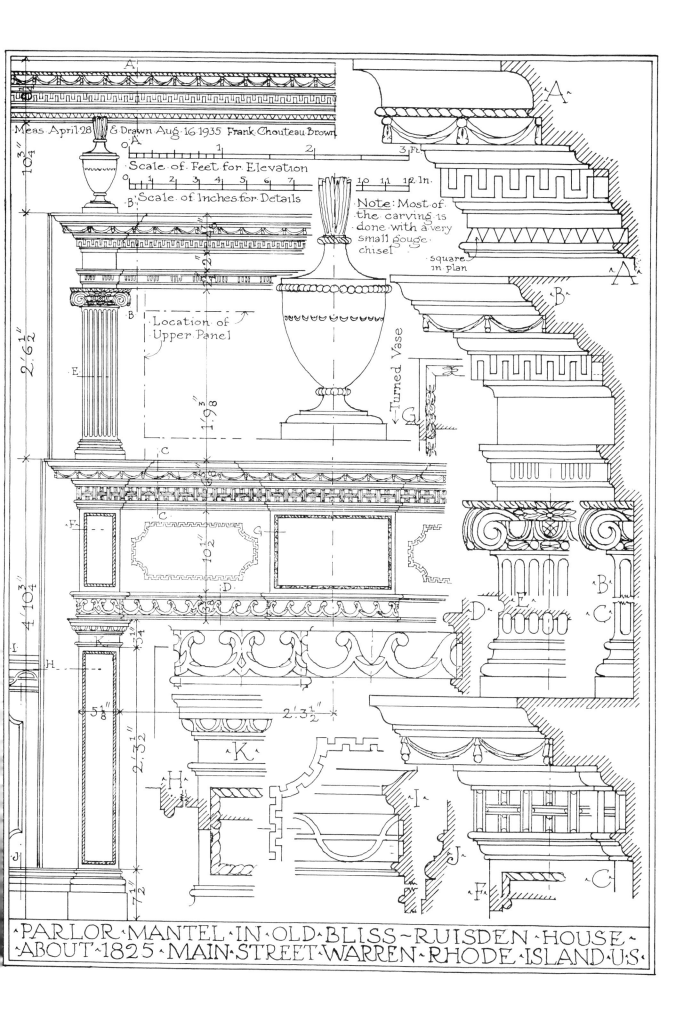

Meas. April 28 & Drawn Aug. 16 1935 Frank Chouteau Brown

Scale of Feet for Elevation

Scale of Inches for Details

Note: Most of the carving is done with a very small gouge chisel.

square in plan

Location of Upper Panel

←Turned Vase

PARLOR·MANTEL·IN·OLD·BLISS~RUISDEN·HOUSE·
·ABOUT·1825·MAIN·STREET·WARREN·RHODE·ISLAND·U·S·

Parlor Mantel
BLISS-RUISDEN HOUSE—1825—MAIN STREET, WARREN, RHODE ISLAND

Parlor Mantel
GREENWOOD-CARR HOUSE — 1820 — WATER STREET, WARREN, RHODE ISLAND

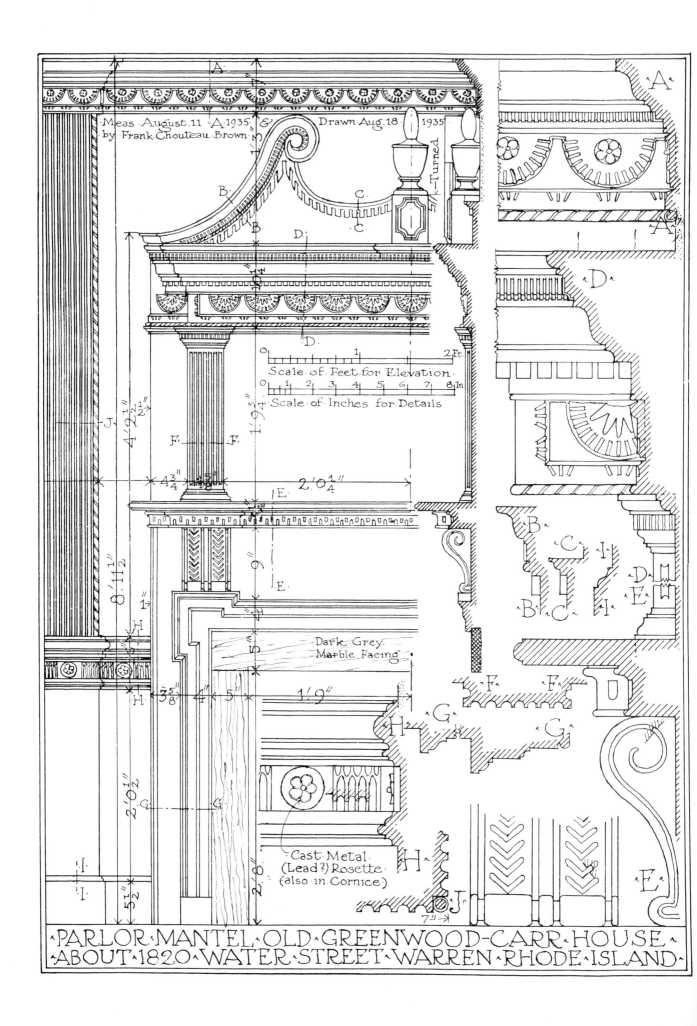

Meas. August 11 A. 1935
by Frank Chouteau Brown

Drawn Aug. 18 1935

Turned

Scale of Feet for Elevation.

Scale of Inches for Details

Dark Grey
Marble Facing

Cast Metal
(Lead?) Rosette
(also in Cornice)

·PARLOR·MANTEL·OLD·GREENWOOD-CARR·HOUSE·
·ABOUT·1820·WATER·STREET·WARREN·RHODE·ISLAND·

HOUSE AT WATER AND WASHINGTON STREETS, WARREN, RHODE ISLAND

HOUSE AT NUMBER 395 WATER STREET, WARREN, RHODE ISLAND

NUMBER 395 WATER STREET

WATER AND WASHINGTON STREETS

DOORWAYS IN WARREN, RHODE ISLAND

Warren, Rhode Island
Part Two

Text by
J. Fenimore Russell
Photographs by
Arthur C. Haskell
Originally published in 1935 as White Pine Monograph
Volume XXI, Number 6

Mantel and Doorway Detail
WATERMAN HOUSE, WARREN, RHODE ISLAND

SOME OLD HOUSES OF WARREN, RHODE ISLAND, PART TWO

RHODE Island had never secured a Royal Charter while the early settlements in the region now known by that name were being established. But in each separate locality the leaders made independent satisfactory arrangements with their predecessors on the land, the Indians then in possession, and set up informally their local community control, without bothering at all about the larger aspects and problems of organizing a "state" government or securing the royal permission of the English King to establish themselves among the colonies of the New World.

But when, under fear of Indian attack, the then existing thirty-nine towns in the colonies of Massachusetts Bay, Plymouth, New Haven, and Connecticut all joined together as a "New England Confederacy," for mutual assistance and protection against the Indians, Dutch, and French — and the settlements within the somewhat uncertain boundaries of what was to become Rhode Island were refused admission — the various settlements then found on what is now Newport Island, and the shores of Narragansett Bay, decided to make common cause and themselves do something about it. As a result of this decision, Roger Williams sailed off to England, where he finally secured a charter from Charles II, dated July 8, 1663 under the name of the Providence Plantations, which covered only the islands and the mainland to the west of Narragansett Bay. The land to the east of the bay was then claimed by the Massachusetts Bay

and Plymouth colonies, as the two Shawomet sachems then living within that district had submitted, and sold the land to them, in 1643. King Charles not only gave Roger Williams the Charter for which he asked but also appointed, as the first Royal Governor, Benedict Arnold of Newport.

The controversy as to the exact boundary line between these groups was already under way at that time (started perhaps by Williams' own first attempt to find residence upon the Blackstone River banks, that would still remain outside the control of the Massachusetts Church communities!) and continued to be a bone of contention between Massachusetts and Rhode Island for over two hundred years!

At last, in 1746, by King's decree, the boundary townships of Warren, Bristol, Little Compton, Tiverton, and Cumberland were declared part of Rhode Island; but even then the final details necessary to complete this transfer were not settled for another hundred and twenty years; and until, in 1862, the Massachusetts part of Pawtucket and the western part of Seekonk (which then became East Providence) were given to Rhode Island, while the land taken from Tiverton and included as the Rhode Island town of Fall River was finally given to Massachusetts.

But long before this, in 1644, the Rev. Samuel Newman, one of the early leaders settling first in the Massachusetts Bay district, with a part of his Weymouth congregation and some familes from Hingham, located upon a ten miles square area of land purchased by the settlers themselves from Massasoit, the Indian chief who then lived within the present boundaries of the town of Warren—but then known as Rehoboth.

In 1746—just after it was set apart from Massachusetts and given to Rhode Island by King's decree —an act of the Rhode Island legislature incorporated Warren as part of Rhode Island; including "that part of territory confirmed to Rhode Island which has heretofore been part of Swansea and Barrington, with a small part of Rehoboth adjoining, with the inhabitants thereof, into a township by the name of Warren."

The town was at that time named for Admiral Sir Peter Warren, who in June of 1745 commanded the English fleet that, with the army of Americans under Sir William Pepperel, had captured Louisburg.

Finally, one more factor should be added to this complicated minor shift of territory, in order that the record may be more complete; and for that purpose it is necessary to return to Great Britain, and start again, over two hundred years earlier.

In 1649, the first year of the Cromwell protectorate, the Rev. John Miles became pastor of a church in Swansea in Glamorganshire, a county in South Wales. In 1663, two years after the restoration of Charles II (and the same year Roger Williams secured the "Plantations" Charter), the "Act of Uniformity" was passed in England—and the Rev. Miles became a "Nonconformist," left Wales, and came to Rehoboth in Plymouth Colony! But even there, his religious views not agreeing with those established and maintained in that colony, he again shortly removed to Wannamoiset in Barrington, at a location that has recently been established as about three miles northwest of Warren.

At this point the first Baptist Meeting House was set up; and a section of land was granted (on Oct. 30, 1667) to the Rev. Miles and his followers, and named Swansea, in honor of the Welsh town from which many of them had come. Its area then also included the present towns of Somerset in Massachusetts, and Warren and Barrington in Rhode Island.

One of the most ingenious and distinctive local developments in the architecture of Warren is the type of mantel whose variations and growth have been well illustrated in this and the preceding chapter. It reached perhaps its final fulfillment in the ornate example from the Waterman House (pages 80, 81, and 82); and its start may perhaps be found in the mantel from the second section of the Miller House, built a score or more of years after the original part, containing the simple earlier mantel shown upon the same pages (86 and 87), was erected in 1789. The intermediate development may be followed through the two examples illustrated in Chapter 4. Along with these mantels, is a local door enframement, with a similar crocheted top pediment.

Along with these local door and mantel details, there has also been developed similar local expressions of detail treatments around the window openings, and upon the design of dados and staircases—as well as a number of sturdily attractive entrance doorway treatments; representative examples of all of which are to be found upon these accompanying and preceding pages. The variations of dado design and treatment are particularly intriguing; especially as they appear in connection with a number of characteristic staircase examples—from this town, as well as from Bristol.

In most of these stair run wall treatments the newel and landing posts are also represented upon the wall face, either in whole or in part—a matter of treatment that is here and there extended to apply even to a duplication of the balusters themselves, in place of the paneling, along the wall boundary of the stair run.

The Waterman House stairway is a case in point. Here a rather simple and sturdy baluster is used, and the fluted newel column is echoed upon the wall opposite, as well as the upper landing posts above. A somewhat similar stair handling appears also in the hallway of the Carr House, although with many differences in the details and proportions of the parts. In a simpler (and later) form the same essential elements are employed in the staircase in the house at 582 Main Street; while, in much cruder and bolder treatment, they may also be found in the earlier built stairs of the Miller House; which may again be compared with a somewhat later example found in the house at 606 Main Street. The last two exhibit a less elaborate stair end bracket; and the latter also shows a simple use of the wall dado pilaster opposite the stair posts, employed with a ramping stair rail and dado cap.

The other marked product of the early houses in this district—and one that has more successfully succeeded in maintaining its original merits, too—is to be seen by any passer-by in the beautiful and varied examples of house doorways.

In all the elaboration of cutting that is particularly exhibited in the interior details and mantels of this district, the ingenuity with which a wide variety of detail treatment and ornamental handling of the mouldings has been obtained by the use of only one or two sizes of hollow gouge chisels must express something of the wide-spread skill in the moulding and carving of wood by the many local carpenters that were probably developed in this region by the boatbuilding industry on the shores of Narragansett Bay.

Two early—and simple—but beautifully proportioned small gambrel cottages typical of many others in this locality are also included in this chapter. All these structures appear to belong to an earlier and less elaborate period. They contain little, if any, "finish" of conventional type; but depend almost exclusively for their appeal upon the excellent proportions of their roof slopes, and their low and hospitable appearance.

Stair and Hall
WATERMAN HOUSE—1820—WATER STREET, WARREN, RHODE ISLAND

Door Enframement

Wainscot
WATERMAN HOUSE — 1820 — WATER STREET, WARREN, RHODE ISLAND

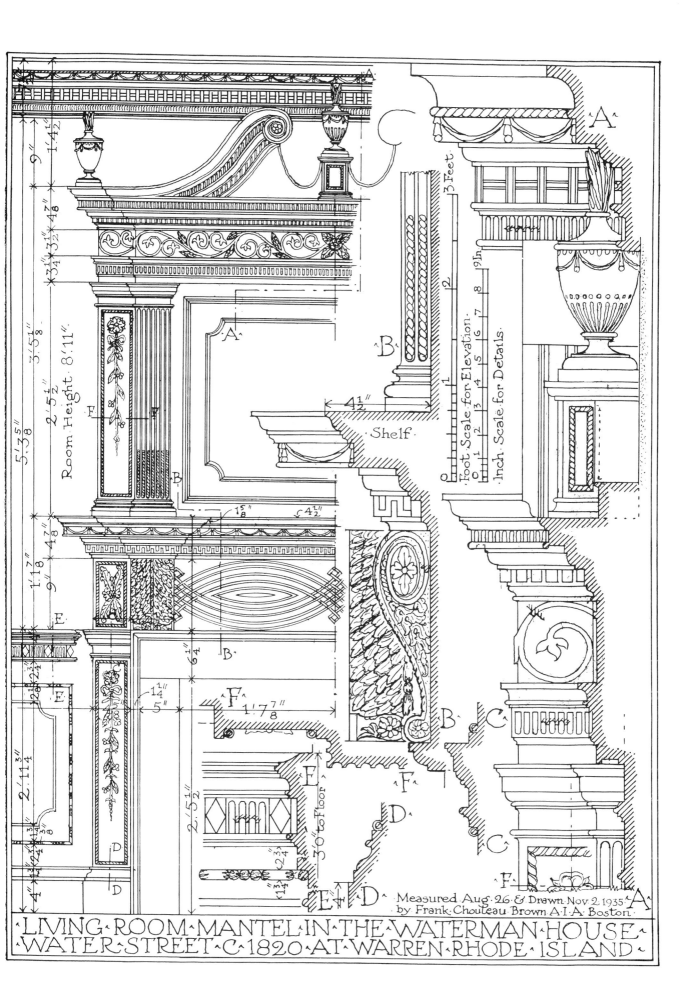

Room Height 8'11"

Shelf

3 Feet

9 In.

Foot Scale for Elevation.

Inch. Scale for Details.

Measured Aug. 26. & Drawn Nov. 2. 1935.
by Frank Chouteau Brown A.I.A. Boston.

LIVING·ROOM·MANTEL·IN·THE·WATERMAN·HOUSE·
WATER·STREET·C·1820·AT·WARREN·RHODE·ISLAND·

Living Room Mantel
WATERMAN HOUSE—1820—WATER STREET, WARREN, RHODE ISLAND

Doorway Detail
CARR HOUSE, 353 WATER STREET, WARREN, RHODE ISLAND

NUMBER 582 MAIN STREET

CARR HOUSE, 353 WATER STREET

CHARACTERISTIC STAIRCASE EXAMPLES, WARREN, RHODE ISLAND

NUMBER 606 MAIN STREET

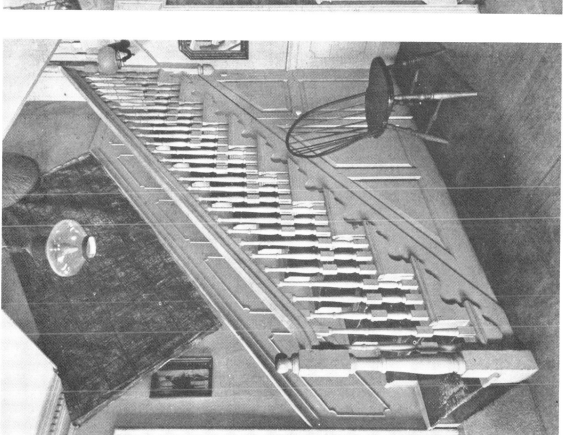

MILLER ABBOT HOUSE

CHARACTERISTIC STAIRCASE EXAMPLES, WARREN, RHODE ISLAND

Built in 1789.

Built about 1805.

MANTELS IN THE MILLER-ABBOT HOUSE, WARREN, RHODE ISLAND

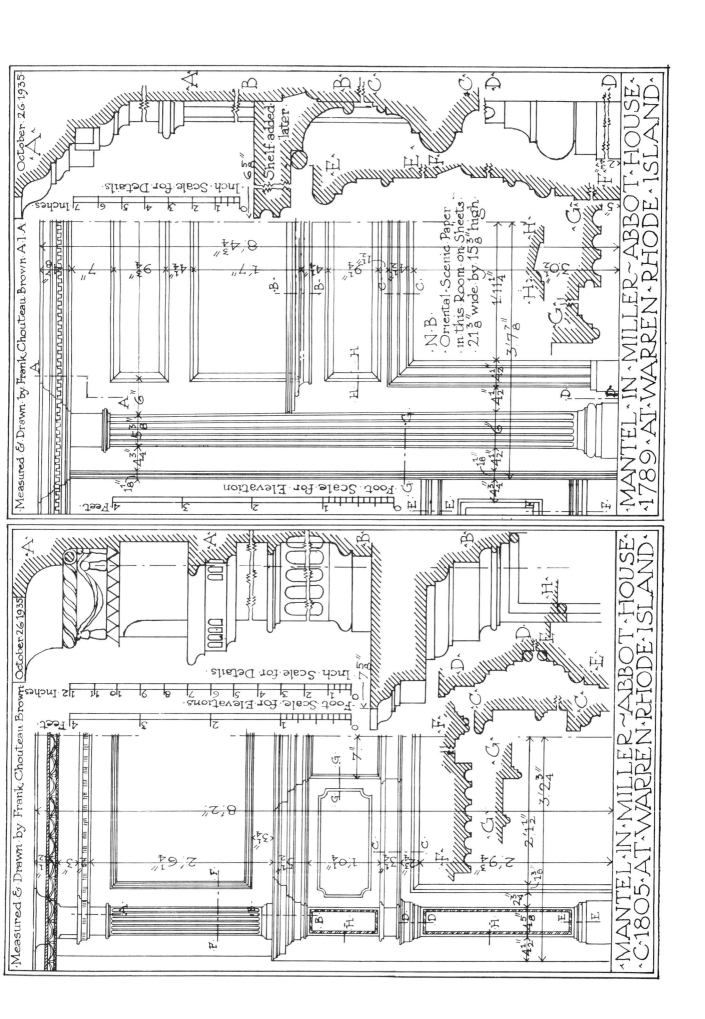

MANTEL·IN·MILLER~ABBOT·HOUSE·
·1789·AT·WARREN·RHODE·ISLAND·

October·26·1935·

Measured·&·Drawn·by·Frank·Chouteau·Brown·A.I.A·

·Inch·Scale·for·Details·

Shelf·added·later

N·B·
·Oriental·Scenic·Paper·
in·this·Room·on·Sheets·
21⅜″·wide·by·15¾″·high.

·Foot·Scale·for·Elevation

MANTEL·IN·MILLER~ABBOT·HOUSE·
·C·1805·AT·WARREN·RHODE·ISLAND·

October·26·1935·

Measured·&·Drawn·by·Frank·Chouteau·Brown·

·Inch·Scale·for·Details·

·Foot·Scale·for·Elevations

NUMBER 23 BROAD STREET, BUILT ABOUT 1750

NUMBER 95 UNION STREET
TYPICAL GAMBREL COTTAGES, WARREN, RHODE ISLAND

Doorway Detail
HOUSE AT NUMBER 41 STATE STREET, WARREN, RHODE ISLAND

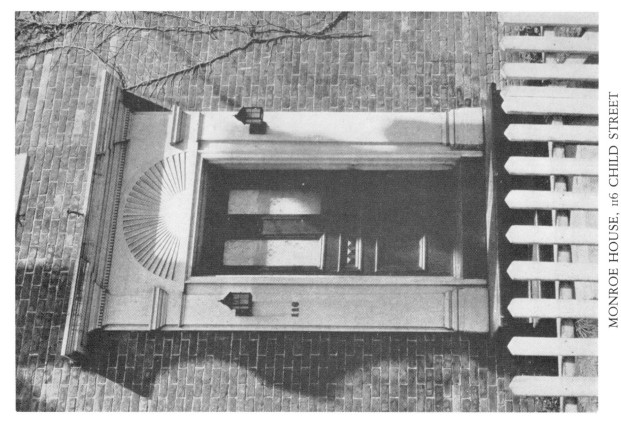

MONROE HOUSE, 116 CHILD STREET

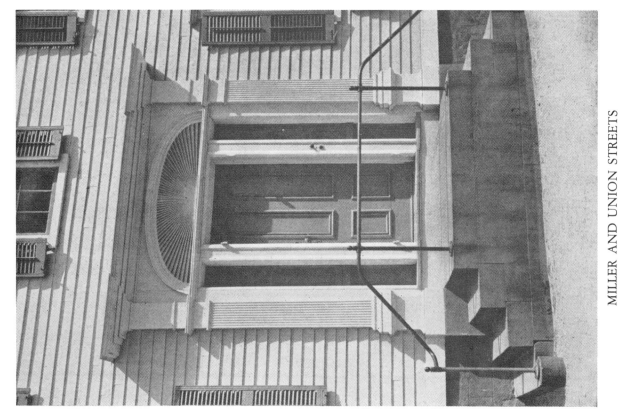

MILLER AND UNION STREETS
EXAMPLES OF HOUSE DOORWAYS IN WARREN, RHODE ISLAND

Little Compton and
Tiverton Four Corners

Text by
John C. Halden
Photographs by
Arthur C. Haskell
Originally published in 1936 as White Pine Monograph
Volume XXII, Number 6

BETTY ALDEN HOUSE, TIVERTON NEAR LITTLE COMPTON, RHODE ISLAND

LITTLE COMPTON AND TIVERTON FOUR CORNERS

THE extreme southern part of the area, now in Rhode Island, and situated between the Massachusetts boundary and the Sakonnet River below the township of Tiverton, is known as Little Compton. It contains a great deal of rolling, rocky upland; a swampy and much indented seacoast; some old farms and fishing settlements; many old houses, and, at the present time, three principal villages. Sakonnet, a small cluster of fishing shacks, small cottages, and modest summer places, is located at the extreme southwestern tip of the area, almost at Sakonnet Point. Adamsville, a small village at the head of a deep sea inlet, of old and new houses, grouped about the old Manchester Store, in the northeasternmost corner of the township. And Little Compton Commons — another very small settlement, almost in the geographical center of the area — and also a mixture of old and new dwellings, a smithy-garage, and a few stores.

Otherwise the township contains much unoccupied and barren land, many Indian sites and burial grounds, a fairly large number of summer cottages, especially along its eastern coastline — and a scattering but surprisingly large number of old homesteads, principally aligned along the main north and south roadway, extending up to Tiverton and Fall River at the north.

In early times all this area was occupied by the Seaconnet tribe of Indians, under Philip of Pokanoket; and Benjamin Church, of Duxbury, a carpenter, is believed to have been the first white settler, in 1674. After King Philip's War, Capt. Church settled in Bristol and died there in 1718. The name is supposed to have been taken from Little Compton, of Oxford-shire, England. The town was incorporated in 1682; and was transferred from Massachusetts to Rhode Island along with four other townships — of which Tiverton was one — in January, 1746–1747. Elizabeth Alden, the first white woman born in New England, died May 31, 1717, when 94 years old, and was buried in the village cemetery. In 1790, the township is recorded as having 1542 white inhabitants — with 23 slaves; which is probably considerably more than its winter population today!

Adamsville is a small group of houses clustered about an old store, at the head of an estuary extending a considerable distance inland from the ocean to the south. It is just below the northern line boundary of Little Compton, in its extreme northeastern corner, and it is necessary to pass through this village in order to reach a portion of the Massachusetts area in the township of Westport.

Among some other items of local interest, it is perhaps most widely known from the fact that the Rhode Island Red breed of fowl originated — or was developed — within the surrounding vicinity, and a large bronze tablet erected in commemoration of that fact may be seen upon an old boulder beside the road nearly opposite the Manchester Store. This old store was built by Ebenezer P. Church, in 1820, and is still in use, with much of the original equipment, and little concession to modern ideas of display of merchandise — as may be gathered from the views made of the exterior late this fall. Ebenezer Church, by the way, is claimed to have been a great-great-uncle of President Franklin D. Roosevelt — which, at this particular date and year, may be an object of rather more than pertinent interest. The store came into the possession of Philip Manchester in 1839, and has ever since been run by some member of that family.

One of the most attractive houses in the local group is a large white structure, overshadowed by huge trees eighty to a hundred feet high, located almost upon the Massachusetts line, a few hundred feet to the east of the store. It dates from about 1818–1825; and two other appealing smaller houses are found nearby, one across the street to the west of the store, and another down the side street leading to the isolated part of Westport.

From this small, quiet village the principal east and west roadway climbs steeply up a hill, past a little stone cottage, and after many turns and twists passes another shrub-embowered small cottage and then enters Little Compton Commons, a somewhat larger group of houses nearly halfway to the shores of the Sakonnet River. Here is located the small but attractive Brownell Cottage, with its divided stairway. There is also a small cemetery nearby containing many old headstones with unique inscriptions, which attracted many tourists to obtain rubbings.

A mile or so north of the Little Compton upper boundary, and near the southern edge of Tiverton, is located Tiverton Four Corners; an intersection of the main north and south roadway with a cross road, that continues to the east and south to pass into Little Compton territory at Adamsville—where it almost as instantly passes *out* of Rhode Island, into Massachusetts!

At this intersection, still marked by two old houses and two stores, is also to be seen, upon the southeast corner, the old Whipping Post—a flat stone slab, only a few inches thick and standing about six feet out of the ground—which was much used by Judge Almy, between 1719 and 1812, according to local tradition, especially for the punishment of slaves. Next adjoining is the oldest store, also long in use as the Post Office, but known as the John Almy House, built in 1797—with a charmingly typical gambrel-roofed cottage just beyond.

Only a few hundred yards beyond this intersection, to the south, is the old Peregrine White grist mill, where old residents brought their grain to be ground into Rhode Island "Johnnie Cake Meal"; and which, according to the sign upon its road front, is still worked two days of each week! Within a short half-mile distance are still to be seen this mill, one of the stores, and no less than four of the old houses built by members of the White family—several of which still house their descendants—the White Homestead, a little south of the mill (and almost upon the Little Compton boundary), has been occupied by at least seven generations of that family. Its original builder was a well

known sea captain on whaling vessels running out of New Bedford. The White family burying ground was located upon this farm and contained, among others, the stone in memory of the child of Peregrine White of the Mayflower (said to be the first born of Mayflower stock), but the old headstones have recently been taken up and removed to the Amicable churchyard, nearby.

Turning west, across a salt water inlet, onto Punkateest Neck, is the Colonel Cooke House, shown as a landmark upon an old map of 1730, which—despite some regrettable Victorian changes—has retained a charming old doorway, the almost unique "stoep" illustrated, and one rarely beautiful interior!

Following on south along this same highway, one passes other old houses overlooking the Sakonnet River, and Newport Island to the west. Here about all the other dwellings shown or mentioned in this chapter are located, including the Oliver H. Almy House, from which a simple but typical mantel has been drawn, and the house of Captain Robert Gray, who discovered the Columbia River, and was the first American to carry the Stars and Stripes around the world. Another historic house is that usually known as the Betty Alden House. The east portion was built in 1682 by William Pabodie to house himself and his wife, Elizabeth Alden—who was the first white woman born in New England. They were among the first settlers, and their descendants occupied the house, until it came into the possession of Col. Pardon Gray, in 1762, when the western part was added. The mantel, here drawn, is in the old fire room of the original house, while the fireplace shown in the photograph is now in the dining room. Nearly across from this dwelling is the home of two other original settlers, Samuel and Mary (Potter) Wilbor, built in 1691, and occupied by eight generations.

The home of William and Sarah (Haywood) Dye, now known as Duffield Farms, is a picturesque and rambling structure, displaying the obvious changes and additions that have been made by many generations of dwellers. The early "block-house" has been almost completely engulfed by these many additions; and while the original portion was built in 1684, by these two "first settlers," it has housed many other well known persons, among them John Gray, a soldier in the American Revolution.

This main highway continues out to the extreme end of the peninsula, to the lighthouse at Sakonnet Point, passing along the way other early houses and cottages, and many newer summer dwellings—particularly in the southwestern portion of the township, overlooking the shores and beaches along the lower Sakonnet River and the ocean.

SAMUEL AND MARY (POTTER) WILBOR HOUSE—1691—LITTLE COMPTON, RHODE ISLAND

OLIVER H. ALMY HOUSE, LITTLE COMPTON, RHODE ISLAND

AMASA GRAY HOUSE, LITTLE COMPTON, RHODE ISLAND

AMASA GRAY HOUSE, LITTLE COMPTON, RHODE ISLAND

Second Floor Mantel

Second Floor Mantel

AMASA GRAY HOUSE, LITTLE COMPTON, RHODE ISLAND

MANCHESTER STORE, ADAMSVILLE, RHODE ISLAND

WHITE HOUSE, ADAMSVILLE, RHODE ISLAND

Detail of Side Doorway
COLONEL COOKE HOUSE, PUNKATEEST NECK, RHODE ISLAND

Old Stoep
COLONEL COOKE HOUSE, PUNKATEEST NECK, RHODE ISLAND

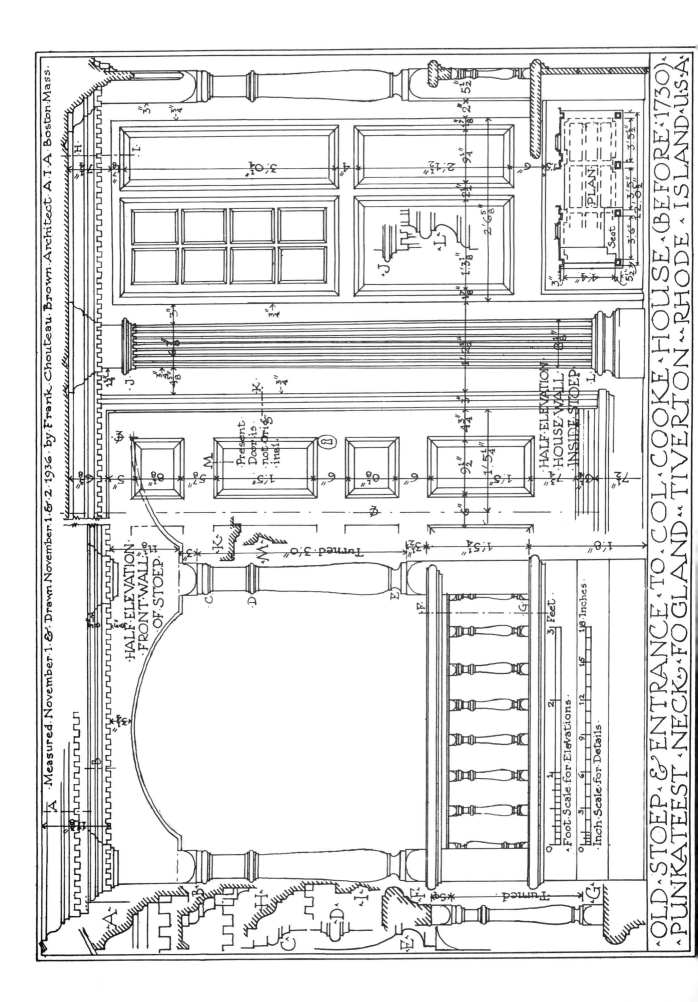

·OLD·STOEP·&·ENTRANCE·TO·COL·COOKE·HOUSE·(BEFORE·1730)·
·PUNKATEEST·NECK·FOGLAND·TIVERTON··RHODE·ISLAND·U.S.A·

·Measured·November·1·&·2·1936··by·Frank·Chouteau·Brown·Architect·A.I.A·Boston·Mass·

·HALF·ELEVATION·FRONT·WALL·OF·STOEP·

·HALF·ELEVATION·HOUSE·WALL·INSIDE·STOEP·

Present Door is not orig inal.

PLAN

Seat

·Foot·Scale·for·Elevations·

·Inch·Scale·for·Details·

3 Feet

18 Inches

OLD STOEP AND ENTRANCE—COL. COOKE HOUSE, PUNKATEEST NECK, RHODE ISLAND

COLONEL COOKE HOUSE—c1730—PUNKATEEST NECK, TIVERTON, RHODE ISLAND

COLONEL COOKE HOUSE—c1730—PUNKATEEST NECK, TIVERTON, RHODE ISLAND

OLIVER H. ALMY HOUSE—1745—LITTLE COMPTON, RHODE ISLAND

WILLIAM PABODIE (BETTY ALDEN HOUSE), LITTLE COMPTON, RHODE ISLAND

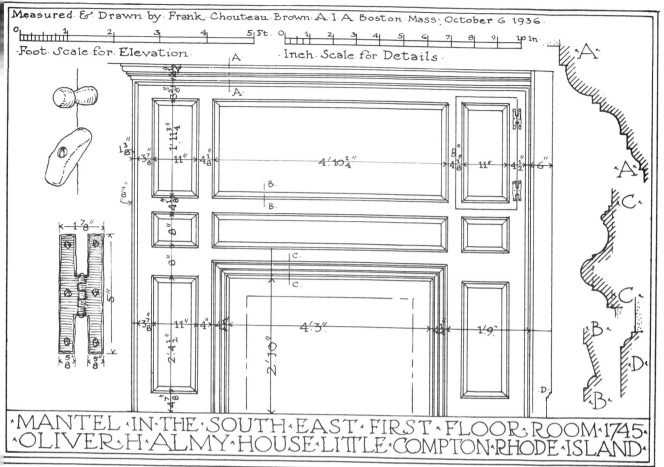

Measured & Drawn by Frank Chouteau Brown A.I.A. Boston Mass. October 6 1936.

·Foot·Scale·for·Elevation·   ·Inch·Scale·for·Details·

·MANTEL·IN·THE·SOUTH·EAST·FIRST·FLOOR·ROOM·1745·
·OLIVER·H·ALMY·HOUSE·LITTLE·COMPTON·RHODE·ISLAND·

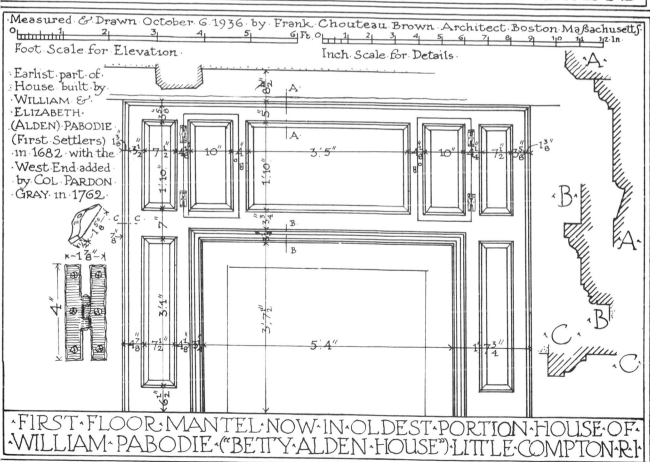

·Earlist·part·of·
·House·built·by·
·WILLIAM·&·
·ELIZABETH·
·(ALDEN)·PABODIE·
·(First·Settlers)·
·in·1682·with·the·
·West·End·added·
·by·COL·PARDON·
·GRAY·in·1762·

·FIRST·FLOOR·MANTEL·NOW·IN·OLDEST·PORTION·HOUSE·OF·
·WILLIAM·PABODIE·("BETTY·ALDEN·HOUSE")·LITTLE·COMPTON·R·I·

BROWNELL COTTAGE, LITTLE COMPTON COMMONS, RHODE ISLAND

Tiverton, Rhode Island

Text by
Roderick H. Parker
Photographs by
Arthur C. Haskell
Originally published in 1936 as White Pine Monograph
Volume XXII, Number 5

Mantel

NATHANIEL BRIGGS HOUSE, TIVERTON, RHODE ISLAND

TIVERTON, RHODE ISLAND, AND SOME OF ITS EARLY DWELLINGS

THE easternmost part of Rhode Island consists of a narrow strip of land contained between the present Massachusetts line upon the east, and bounded by the waterways of the Sakonnet River and Mount Hope Bay upon the west. From Providence, it can only be reached by land, by passing through a considerable part of Massachusetts and the city of Fall River; although there exist two bridges, one of recent construction over a portion of Mount Hope Bay, that connects Newport Island with the mainland at the southern extremity of Bristol, and another older bridge over a narrow part of the Sakonnet River, that connects Newport Island with Tiverton.

Tiverton is the name given to the northernmost part of this strip of Rhode Island territory, while its southern portion is known as Little Compton. In area it is between nine and ten miles long from north to south, and only about three and a half miles wide; and the principal settlements are known as North Tiverton, Tiverton, and Tiverton Four Corners.

The old connection with Newport Island is at about the middle of its length, at Tiverton; while just south of this center is an almost landlocked inlet named Nanaquaket Pond — and most of the oldest houses are to be found along the old waterfront road.

Most of the local names found in this region are of Indian origin; this entire section having been called by them Pocasset. At the time of the King Philip war, it was governed by Queen Weetamoe (a name that has recently become familiar from having been used for one of the America Cup defenders) who was then at the head of all the Pocasset tribes. In 1680 the Plymouth colonists purchased this region from the Indians, who then sold it to Edward Gray and seven other Englishmen for the sum of £1200 (about $3670.00); and Tiverton was incorporated as a town in 1694. During the Revolution, Tiverton Heights was occupied by a large camp of American soldiers.

What is probably the oldest remaining house in all this region is still to be seen at the edge of the garden in the rear of the David Durfee House, on the eastern side of the main roadway, a little to the south of Nanaquaket Pond. A long, low, narrow, one-story stone masonry building, it had most of its interior work removed many years ago and was used as a wood shed or storehouse for a considerable time. It had originally probably only two rooms, the separating partition being at the right of the center doorway, as viewed from the eastern or garden side. While the exact date of this simple structure is unknown, it undoubtedly belongs to very early in 1700.

In front of this oldest dwelling stands the David Durfee House, built in 1768, which has been especially well maintained by its recent owners; as should appear from the views reproduced, although it has now an extension to the south of more recent date. The doorway is one of several of a very similar type that may be seen in this region; and is distinctive because of its extreme height and narrow proportions. The example that appears upon another Durfee homestead, standing a little further to the north, has been measured — as it displays some extremely delicate details more un-

JOHN GRAY HOUSE, NANAQUAKET, TIVERTON, RHODE ISLAND

usual and locally characteristic than the earlier example on the David Durfee dwelling. This house is a later development of the same type, and was built by either the next—or perhaps even the second following—generation of the same family.

A little further to the south, standing back at the end of an old avenue of trees, is one of the most interesting of the houses remaining in this whole region. Known generally as the Nathaniel Briggs House, it was built probably previous to 1777. As it now stands, the portion facing south upon the old garden is the oldest part; the northern service end having been built to

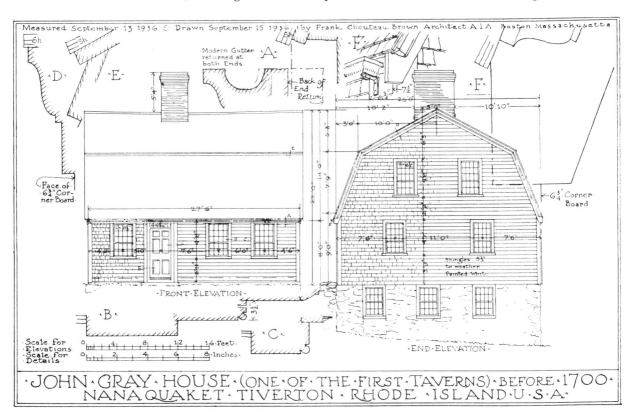

NATHANIEL BRIGGS HOUSE AND GARDEN, TIVERTON, RHODE ISLAND

Side Doorway

South Doorway

NATHANIEL BRIGGS HOUSE, TIVERTON, RHODE ISLAND

NATHANIEL BRIGGS HOUSE, TIVERTON, RHODE ISLAND

replace the earlier kitchen and service quarters, which were in an extreme state of disrepair through long neglect. In the process of this replacement the original staircase was lost, as well as the large and spacious arrangement of the old kitchen, planned for the period when slaves were available as the family retainers of that region. A new room was also added to the south front of the house at its western end; but most of the structure that may be seen in the photographs taken from the lower terraced garden is the original house, except what changes have been made in the wall covering and in the attic story. At one time the

The entrance doorway design of this dwelling is another of the very unusual and architecturally interesting local types. While more elaborate, it contains some of the same elements—particularly the suggestion of pilasters on each side of the opening framework, that are attached with no relation to any supported entablature, which are also found in the details of the doorway of the old weathered house at Tiverton Center, built by a local carpenter, Caleb Cory, for the first owner, John Cooke, which has been shown in one of the measured drawings. This dwelling was built before 1775, and its older mouldings and clapboards, upon the

Interior
NATHANIEL BRIGGS HOUSE, TIVERTON, RHODE ISLAND

property of Lt.-Gov. Oliver, the place was confiscated at the time he fled to England. It is now one of the few remaining old manor houses of the region that reflected in New England something of the vanished life and atmosphere of the old plantations along the southern Atlantic coast, and thus perhaps somewhat explains and justifies the old name originally given this state in its charter—the Providence Plantations!

western front, which have been exposed to the weather during all these years, without surface protection of any kind, are worn almost to wafer thinness at some places along the lower wall near the watertable. The heavy hewn plank window caps on this building are also to be noted as unusually sturdy in type.

The Samuel West House, at Acushnet Center, was built at least as early as 1810–1815; while there are

OLD DURFEE HOUSE — 1810–1818 — NANAQUAKET, TIVERTON, RHODE ISLAND

JOHN COOKE HOUSE—c1775—TIVERTON, RHODE ISLAND

THOMAS OSBORN HOUSE, NORTH TIVERTON, RHODE ISLAND

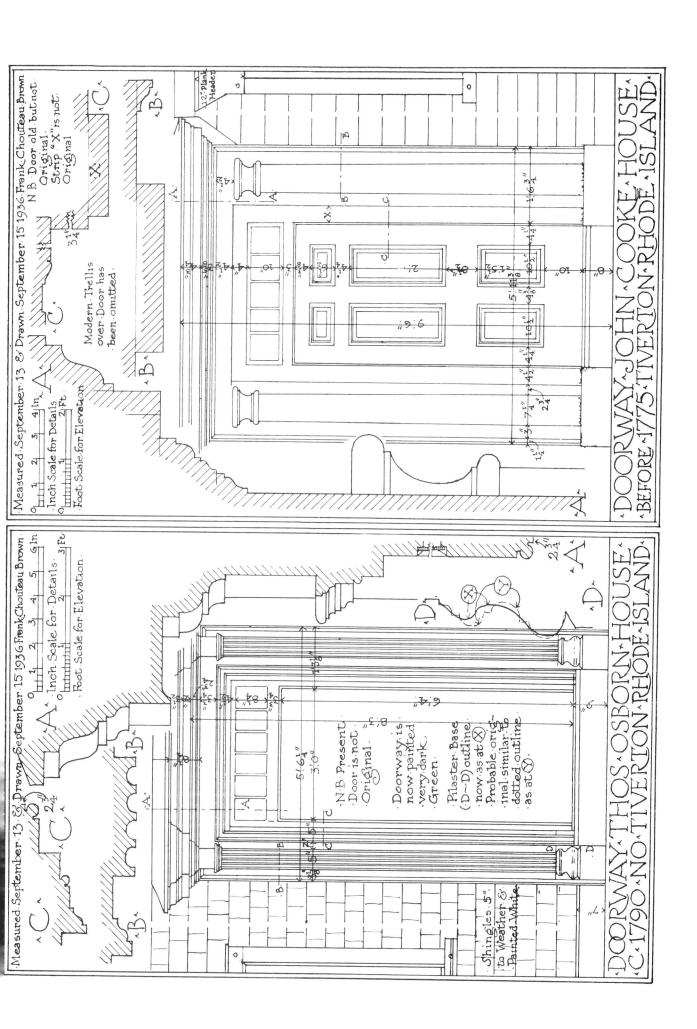

Measured·September·13·&·Drawn·September·15·1936·Frank·Choteau·Brown.

N·B·Door·old·but·not·Original·
Strip·"X"·is·not·Original

Modern·Trellis·over·Door·has·been·omitted.

Inch·Scale·for·Details·
Foot·Scale·for·Elevation.

·DOORWAY·JOHN·COOKE·HOUSE·
·BEFORE·1775·TIVERTON·RHODE·ISLAND·

Measured·September·13·&·Drawn·September·15·1936·Frank·Choteau·Brown.

·N·B·Present·Door·is·not·Original.

·Doorway·is·now·painted·very·dark·Green.

·Plaster·Base·(D~D)·outline·now·as·at·X.·Probable·orig~inal·similar·to·dotted·outline·as·at·Y.

Shingles·5"·to·Weather·&·Painted·White.

Inch·Scale·for·Details·
Foot·Scale·for·Elevation.

·DOORWAY·THOS·OSBORN·HOUSE·
·C·1790·NO·TIVERTON·RHODE·ISLAND·

JOHN COOKE HOUSE—BEFORE 1775—TIVERTON, RHODE ISLAND

SAMUEL WEST HOUSE—1810-1815—ACUSHNET CENTER, RHODE ISLAND

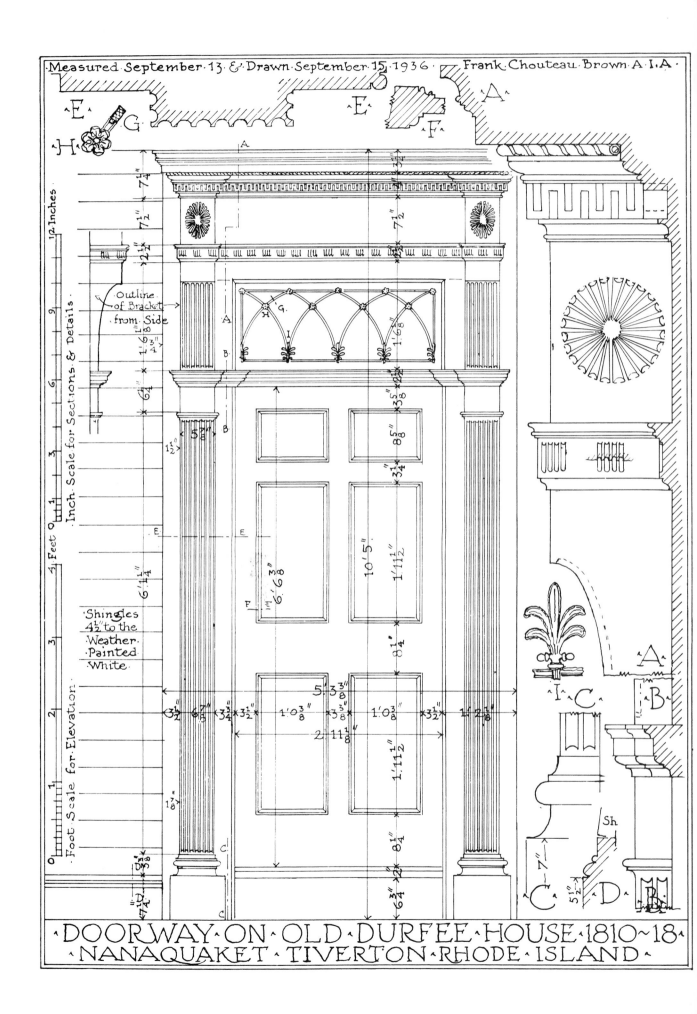

Measured September 13 & Drawn September 15 1936 · Frank Chouteau Brown A.I.A

·DOORWAY·ON·OLD·DURFEE·HOUSE·1810~18·
·NANAQUAKET·TIVERTON·RHODE·ISLAND·

some details that would seem to suggest that it was —
in part, at least — of a considerably older vintage. But
in its exterior doorway, as it now appears in these photographs, it would seem to suggest the kind of design
and details that were favored by the carpenters and
builders of the first years of the nineteenth century.
Yet in many ways it expresses less individuality and
character than most of the other examples of local
dwellings that have been placed within this region.
Samuel West came across the peninsula from Dart-
mouth early in 1800, and was a divine at the time;
but whether he then built the house now known by

the area enclosed by the trim of the doorway is
bounded by a moulding extending up the two sides and
mitred to turn across the top of the door frame below
the cornice, just as in the door treatments of the
Briggs and Cooke houses; although, in this case, it dies
out against the sides of the pilaster caps and bed-
mouldings of the cornice.

Of course, there are many other smaller and less
important types of dwellings also, scattered all about
this Tiverton region, of which the old John Gray
House is one of the oldest. Dating from about 1700,
it was first used as a tavern, one of the earliest in

JAMES OTIS HAMBY COTTAGE, TIVERTON, RHODE ISLAND

his name, or purchased and enlarged a smaller dwelling
already upon the land, is not known.

Another old house is the one at North Tiverton,
known as the Thomas Osborn Homestead. Again the
date of construction is not established; but the Osborn
referred to lived between 1766 and 1833; and much
of the moulding detail about the dwelling suggests it to
be very definitely of the period preceding the beginning
of the nineteenth century. Oddly enough, the projec-
tions shown in the cornice over this doorway have no
relation whatsoever to the side pilasters, below, while
— with these pilasters removed — it would be noted that

the region, and was also the home of the seven
Church brothers, although so great a number would
have seemed somewhat to crowd its modest dimensions. Set in its unusual site, upon the borders of a
little fishing inlet, the grace and charm of its beautifully proportioned and spacious gambrel roof ends
can be fully seen and appreciated. Besides, there are
a number of the so-called Cape Cod cottage types
along this shoreline; such as the James Otis Hamby
Cottage, and many others; but they do not possess that
local quality and distinction that has been used as a
final means of selection for most of our illustrations.

THOMAS OSBORN HOMESTEAD — c1790 — NORTH TIVERTON, RHODE ISLAND

Providence, Rhode Island

Text by
Norman M. Isham
Photographs by
Julian A. Buckley
Originally published in 1918 as White Pine Monograph
Volume IV, Number 3

Detail of Front

COLONEL JOSEPH NIGHTINGALE HOUSE — 1792 — PROVIDENCE, RHODE ISLAND

PROVIDENCE AND ITS COLONIAL HOUSES

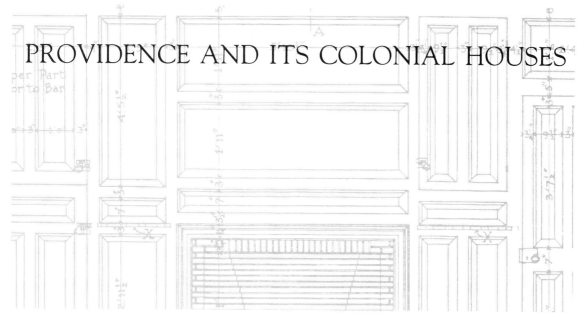

NEARLY every man and boy in eighteenth-century Rhode Island turned, early or late, to blue water. Sailor or fisherman, sea captain or merchant, they all drew their living or their wealth from the ocean, and even the great cotton spinning industry of the early nineteenth century was sustained, in its beginnings, by fortunes made on the sea.

The wealth which this traffic brought to all the older ports of the colonies was reflected in their building, and Providence, as a busy harbor, has a heritage of Colonial houses which, if it is not so well known as that of Salem or Portsmouth — indeed, it is scarcely known at all outside of Rhode Island itself and imperfectly there — may still claim to rival that of the others and, in some ways, to surpass it.

The town was settled on the slope of a high, steep hill, and at the foot of the hill a straggling street, following the shore of the river. This, the present North and South Main Street, still exists. Here stood the houses of the early town, with one room only, or with two rooms side by side and a great stone chimney at the end of the building toward the hill. A dwelling of this kind still forms a part of the eastern end of the Pidge House, on North Main Street, the end at the right of the front door.

Across the river was a narrow neck of land, quite marshy, even an island at some stages of the tide, along which went the Indian trail to the Narragansett and the Pequot countries.

There were no houses on this western bank till the opening of the eighteenth century, when the quaint cottages of the preceding age of farmers began to give way, from age, fire and change of fashion, to the finer, more classic dwellings of the now predominant trading class.

One of the survivors of these early dwellings of the newer type is the Christopher Arnold House, on South Main Street, built about 1735. It has a central chimney against which the stairs in the narrow entry are placed. There is a room on each side of this entry, while behind the chimney is the kitchen with a smaller room at each end. The doorway is the oldest in Providence, as, indeed, the house is the oldest now standing on the Towne Street. The almost Jacobean character of the rosette and the flower on its stalk was probably carried over from the carving on the older furniture. The overhang in the gable is noticeable. This may have been brought about in the same way as the similar overhang in the house which once stood next to this on the north — by building up on the end cornices of a hip-roofed house. That is to say, Providence once had its quota of the hip roofs of the early part of the century, like those still to be seen in Portsmouth and in Newport.

Another house of about 1740, also with a gable overhang, is the Crawford, further north, on the opposite or east side of the street. This has a very remarkable door with large, bent-over leaves above the caps of its pilasters, and the curious bending up of the back band in the middle of the lintel, a characteristic of early work which seems to be a reminiscence of the school of Sir Christopher Wren. Doors like this are rare.

The only other I know is in Hadley. They are derived from some of the bracketed English forms.

The central chimney plan which has just been described remained in fashion almost up to the Greek Revival, though the houses grew larger, lost their quaintness and acquired more dignity. Dwellings of the type were built even after 1800. The plan was no longer the tip of the fashion, however. The second quarter of the century,

CHRISTOPHER ARNOLD HOUSE — c1735 —
SOUTH MAIN STREET, PROVIDENCE, RHODE ISLAND

especially the years just before 1750, and, of course, even more the years just before the Revolution, when the money from privateering in the Old French War was flowing into the town, saw the rise and spread here, as in the rest of New England, of the central-entry type of plan — that in which a long hall runs through the

house from front to back, with two rooms on each side. Most of the houses of this kind in Providence are of brick; the wooden house of early date on that plan is not common. At any rate, it has not survived in any numbers. It is to be seen in its glory, for Rhode Island, in Newport and not in Providence. The great house at the corner of North Main Street and Branch Avenue may be of this date, as may the Olney Tavern at the corner of Olney Street, once Olney's Lane; but, as a rule, the houses seem simply to have been a larger and finer grade of the central chimney scheme, with more elaborate interior woodwork which is often very excellent.

There was little building in Providence during the Revolution — there was too much distress

View from Southwest

PIDGE HOUSE, NORTH MAIN STREET (PAWTUCKET AVENUE), PROVIDENCE

East End, circa 1700; West End, circa 1745.

in the community for that. The British were at Newport a large part of the time, and the whole colony was an armed camp. When once the struggle was over the town came into a period of great prosperity. Before the war it had been the smaller place, Newport the larger and more important as well as the more wealthy. Now the British occupation had ruined Newport and Providence forged ahead. The earlier trade, which had provided the wherewithal to

Detail of Doorway
CRAWFORD HOUSE — c1740 — SOUTH MAIN STREET

build houses like the Crawford and the Arnold, was with the West Indies. Now the East Indies were levied upon, and the trade with them and China employed a fleet of ships and enriched many merchants, some of whom succeeded in

holding what they acquired in this lucrative traffic while others had the opportunity of musing on the fickleness of fortune.

The houses of this time are often three stories in height, though two is still the common number, and after 1815 the three-story house is rarely built. The rooms are much larger and higher in the greater three-deckers, and in all dwellings the distance "between joints" increases considerably. There is generally a garden door on one side, sometimes with a porch, and the projecting porch on the front comes into fashion. Sometimes the porch has tall columns, and the piazza with the same "colossal orders" is not unknown.

About 1800 — earlier in brick houses — a new

CAPTAIN GEORGE BENSON HOUSE — c1786 — NORTH SIDE OF ANGELL STREET
Now the Grosvenor House

BURROUGH HOUSE—c1820—NORTH SIDE OF POWER STREET

BOSWORTH HOUSE—c1820—EAST SIDE OF COOKE STREET

arrangement appears in the plan. The central-entry type just described had generally only two chimneys, one between the two rooms of the pair on each side of the entry, or hall, as we should call it. The new plan put a chimney in the outer wall of each room. This brought the fireplace nearly opposite the entrance to the room from the hall and left two walls free of windows and even of doors for the furniture. These houses are often three stories high, but the majority are of two stories.

house in Providence and one of the best in the colonies, a great credit to its unknown designer, stands on a lot a little to the north of that on which John Jones Clark, the other partner in the firm of Clark and Nightingale, had already built a large three-story house, long ago destroyed by fire. It was the last word in monumental house-work in its day. It marks the end of a period, too, for almost everything that comes after it is lighter in detail and presents no such appearance of weight and character as this.

JASON WILLIAMS-CROUCH HOUSE — c1800 — NORTH SIDE OF GEORGE STREET

The finest wooden specimen of the great three-storied mansion with the central entry and interior chimneys is the house which Colonel Joseph Nightingale built in 1792 (frontispiece and illustration on page 132) on the east side of the new thoroughfare, called Benefit Street, which ran along parallel to the Main Street about half way up the hill, and which received its name because it was to be a great relief to the congested old village on the waterside. If the street is crooked it is because it had to respect the old family burial grounds — one of them still exists — which lay in its path.

This magnificent dwelling, the best wooden

The house has a fine front porch with the usual brownstone steps and platform, all in front of a central mass which projects slightly from the main body of the façade. The door has a toplight and sidelights, one of the earliest instances of the use of them. Over the porch is a Palladian window, while the window over this again, in the third story, is plain like the others on that floor. Above the cornice of the projecting central motive is a pediment the tympanum of which is filled with glass. There are heavy bevelled quoins at the corners, and the windows have them also, with rusticated voussoirs in their flat arches above which are moulded cor-

COLONEL JOSEPH NIGHTINGALE HOUSE—1792—EAST SIDE OF BENEFIT STREET

Later owned by John Carter Brown, one of whose descendants still possesses it.

EDWARD DEXTER HOUSE — c1799 — NORTH SIDE OF WATERMAN STREET

Now owned by Dr. Day

nices. The main cornice is very well profiled and is in good proportion to the whole height. Even the fronts of the Palladian modillions are carved.

The roof is hipped, as is the case with all the houses of this type, and is surmounted by a small curb which is roofed with gables, of which that in the front, at least, has a glazed tympanum. The balustrade of the main roof has regular balusters with top and bottom rails and posts capped with well-shaped urns. The upper roof has a balustrade of Chinese pattern; that is, with plain sticks between the rails, intersecting in a pattern.

The house was originally square with three rooms on the north side of the entry. The additions on the south are later. There was probably a garden door here as there was in the Clark House, perhaps with a porch, too, as Clark had.

Another firm of merchants was Snow and Munro. Snow had a town house which stood on Westminster Street, but which is now removed to a much less dignified street behind its old location and has become a storehouse after enjoying the high estate of a laundry. It is still an imposing wreck, although raised in the air and shorn of its front door, its chimneys and its balustrades.

An even more interesting house was that which Snow built for his country home, out on the Cranston road, about two miles from the Great Bridge, from which all distances were reckoned in Providence. This had very light detail, with tall slim columns for its front porch, which was of the whole height of the house, and others, equally tall, for the piazzas, of which there was one on each side of the building. It fell into disuse and was pulled down some years ago.

To go back a little, when Captain George Benson retired from the firm of Brown, Benson and Ives, he built the house which stills stands at the top of the hill on the north side of Angell Street and which ranks among the two-story houses of the town at the end of the eighteenth century as its contemporary, the Nightingale, does among those of three stories. Here is the porch on its brownstone platform, and here is the garden door also. The influence of the steep hill on the treatment of Providence houses is well illustrated, too. We shall see it again, later, in the Dorr House (illustrated at top of page 135). The balustrade on this roof is of the regular baluster type, a characteristic of all these larger houses.

Another Providence merchant, Edward Dexter, built on George Street the house now on Waterman Street, owned by Dr. Day. The building was sawed in two and each half moved up the hill, separately, to the present location, where they were reunited. Any one who is skeptical — the moving took place within the memory of men now living — may see the saw-cut in the entablature of the porch.

In this house, built in 1799, we find pilasters used to support the gable at the cornice level in the center of the façade, a treatment of which there is but one other example in Providence. The corners of the house have the ordinary quoins. The windows are surmounted each by an entablature and pediment. The balustrade here differs from those previously described in having alternate blocks of balusters and solid panels. The balusters come over the windows, the panels over the piers.

It will be noted that the house is of the exterior chimney type — that is, the fireplaces are on the outer walls of the rooms — with the usual rather flat hip roof. One cannot help seeing, too, the delicacy of the detail, the lightness of it all as compared with that of the Benson House.

Another four-room exterior-chimney house, of somewhat simpler type, is the Diman House on Angell Street, built by Ebenezer Knight Dexter in 1800 or 1801. The sun parlor and the porch are, of course, modern. The old doorway had been removed, and that now in place was taken from a beautiful summer house which once stood in the old garden.

Of the simpler dwellings one very interesting example is the Bosworth House on Cooke Street, a straightforward solution of its problem, with excellent proportions and quiet detail, much of which is concentrated upon the doorway, which, with its rusticated elliptical arch and jambs, is a recognized type among Providence entrances.

An even simpler house standing on Power Street, very near the Bosworth, is the Burrough House, with its monitor roof and still another type of doorway quite common about 1820.

These Providence doors are sometimes criticized as too much alike, because we do not have here the elaborate late porches of Salem. Porches, it is true, are not common here. They exist, as the photographs of this article show, but they are few in number. The reproach, however, comes from lack of observation. There are many types of doorway, all interesting, and the different examples of each type vary more than might be supposed.

There are doors without the orders, though

SULLIVAN DORR HOUSE — c1810 — PROVIDENCE, RHODE ISLAND

PADELFORD HOUSE — c1815 — SOUTH SIDE OF BENEVOLENT STREET

Doorway

HOUSE ON CHESTNUT STREET,
PROVIDENCE, RHODE ISLAND

they are not common. The Williams-Crouch House has almost the only really classical one, and that is not early. It has merely the architrave, with crossettes, the frieze and pediment, but these elements are very simply and beautifully combined.

Then there are the doors with the orders—columns or pilasters. The oldest of these—it is one of the oldest in the colonies—is that in the Arnold House. I know of nothing just like it, though a leaf and rosette of the same type occur in the interior of a house in southern Rhode Island. This type ruled till after 1800 and lingered in a modified form till 1820 or 1825. The early examples have an entablature above the lintel, with or without a pediment. Generally the order has a pedestal with a panel the top of which is curved. As a rule, there are glazed lights immediately over the door and these were sometimes of bull's-eye glass—that is, were cut from the centers of crown glass sheets. A door at the top of Constitution Hill had these—the last specimens in Providence—till a fire destroyed them a few years ago. The back band of the architrave is, in these oldest doors, turned up in the center of the frieze. Later the frieze

follows Palladio and takes the cushion form.

After a time the round toplight with fan tracery comes into use, and the entablature is done away with over the door opening, while it remains above the columns or pilasters, and the arch is thus allowed to come up into what would be the tympanum. This entablature over the pilaster is sometimes very elaborate, as in the two instances on Arnold Street.

Another doorway, on the same street, has brackets over its narrow panelled pilasters. Over all is the usual entablature and pediment. There is one doorway similar to this on Arnold Street, and one on North Main, but neither is as good. These seem to be the only examples of a rare and very interesting type.

On the corner of Benefit and Bowen streets stands the house built by Sullivan Dorr in 1810 or 1811, and now owned by Mrs. Sayles. (Illustrated at top of page 135.) It varies somewhat even from the late line of Colonial work which we have been following, but perhaps for that very reason, it is of great interest.

The house consisted, originally, of a main

Doorway

CHRISTOPHER ARNOLD HOUSE,
SOUTH MAIN STREET, PROVIDENCE

Doorway and Tracery
DODGE HOUSE, GEORGE STREET
PROVIDENCE, RHODE ISLAND

its clustered columns made to represent Gothic piers and the delicate cusped work in the architrave. Equally interesting — indeed, more so — is the translation of the staid Palladian window into terms of clustered columns and cusped ornament. The effect on the whole is excellent, a commentary on what good proportion will do for a design.

The coves in the cornice are of composition, highly ornamented with an incised pattern. The balustrade, too, is worked out in a manner which is different from the ordinary and which accords with the house. The centerpiece cannot be original.

In all these houses we can see that the standard of workmanship was very high in Providence; as it was, indeed, in all Rhode Island. The details, too, are generally very correct and well designed. There is evidence all through the work in the city that skilful and painstaking workmen wrought upon the building of its homes. What they have left behind them ranks high in the architecture of the old Thirteen Colonies.

block which had a central motive and two short wings. The present addition to this is readily discerned in the photograph. Attached to one side of this main body was an ell to which, in turn, were joined the sheds and, further on, at right angles, the stable and carriage house.

As the block faced south the length lay east and west, that is, against the slope of the hill. The problem was to adjust the various parts of the house and its dependencies to the rather steep grade. This was done with great skill. The house was set well above the street and a high wall of cut granite, pierced by a flight of steps at the gate and crowned by a wooden fence, was built to retain the level of the garden terrace in front of the main part of the building. The floor of the main house and that of the ell are on the same level, but the underpinning of the house is high, while that of the ell is very low, so that the courtyard level is above that of the garden and is reached by a flight of steps through the fence which separates the two. The hill was cut away to allow this court to extend as well as to gain a place for the stable group, which is backed up against the slope, so that its second story is but little above the ground on the uphill side.

The porch of the house is very striking, with

Doorway
SOUTH SIDE OF ARNOLD STREET — c1800 —
PROVIDENCE, RHODE ISLAND

EBENEZER KNIGHT DEXTER HOUSE — c1800 — NORTH SIDE OF ANGELL STREET

North Smithfield, Rhode Island

Text by
M. S. Franklin
Photographs by
Arthur C. Haskell
Originally published in 1935 as White Pine Monograph
Volume XXI, Number 4

Porch and Doorway
WALTER ALLEN HOUSE, UNION VILLAGE, RHODE ISLAND

THE HOUSES AND VILLAGES OF NORTH SMITHFIELD, RHODE ISLAND

FOLLOWING up the valley of the Blackstone River — at one time agriculturally fertile; but during the last one hundred years even more fertile in the close crowding mills and villages that line both its steep-pitched boundaries — from the bay head at Providence toward the north; one comes finally to that point where it passes from the present state of Rhode Island over the Massachusetts boundary, at Woonsocket. Woonsocket itself is a busy mill community, unevenly perched upon these same steep, slippery banks; its area covering hardly even the present populous and built-up sections of the place, which is spilling over its limits into the neighboring townships for much of its residential suburbs.

Of the surrounding territory, the largest part of that most conveniently adjacent, is now called North Smithfield — although both the Smithfields (and a considerably larger area besides) — were all once part of a single considerably larger township. To the east, the township of Cumberland — once itself a small part of a former populous section of Massachusetts, that early in 1800 lacked only one vote of providing the site for the State Capitol; but now incorporated into Rhode Island — also takes part of this same population overflow. But the several village centers still to be found in this area owe nothing to this recent upstart of the northern boundary, but had their origins in, and still remain to testify to, the early growth of industrialism in this portion of New England.

Of these villages, the three most northern ones are situated upon a tributary to the Blackstone, known as Branch River; that, along with *its* tributary, the Chepachet, is fed by the many large lakes or ponds contained within the northwestern townships of Rhode Island, of which only those along the extreme edge of the state toward Connecticut drain westward into the Quinebaug River, which in its turn flows down into the Thames. These villages — along with Glendale, Mohegan and Nasonville; all in the township of Burrillville, just to the west — are Slatersville, Forestdale, and Union Village.

Possibly, too, the little village of Manville — hardly a mile over the eastward boundary of North Smithfield into Lincoln — should almost be included within this group, geographically. It resembles them in age, is laid out with a semblance of *arranged* disposition of its units (what would today be termed "Town Planning" — with two capitals, at least!) around a small central Green, and has its Church placed as an important central element of its plan. If anything, despite the steep inclination of its site toward the swift-running Blackstone River, it possesses perhaps more general relation to the idea of "planning," that has within only the last dozen years come to be accepted on this continent — whence it was derived from the European mill villages and industrial communities, that began to develop in England from about forty years ago — than its sister community of Slatersville; with which we are the more immediately concerned in this chapter.

But to turn first to the consideration of Union Village — which cannot even be found upon the official state highway map! Although now being developed — not to say "overwhelmed" — as merely one of the residential suburbs of Woonsocket; Union Village was one of the comparatively early settlements made in this region, at a time when it was not yet evident that a large part of the population of the section was to derive a living from the early industrial demands of New England, and the power that was to be supplied from the Blackstone River. So it is found located upon a sightly hilltop; with its few remaining old houses divided by the busy thoroughfare of a modern concrete roadway; over which the hurried traveler might easily pass without the realization that the locality possessed any age or interest derived from early associations or settlement.

Its oldest tavern still stands; with openings boarded—a huge hulk, at one end of the village, frowning north along the road; but unless some worthy use is soon found for it, it may not much longer succeed in defying conditions imposed both by weather and economy.

Aside from the old Arnold Tavern, the exterior of the Judge Carpenter House retains some of its original appearance; although changing ownerships and conditions have effected their accustomed results upon the interior. The Walter Allen House, nearby, is one that retains the interior in better state of originality than is usual; although the work, dating from 1802, is expressive of the thinner and more delicate character that is usually found in woodwork of a dozen or fifteen years later. Not far away from the Allen House, down the side street, and a little to its rear, is the building that was the first bank of the region—now made over into a small dwelling. It originally stood on the corner of the main street, from which position it has been removed to its present location. The change in use, has naturally also resulted in considerable changes in structure—both inside and out—and it now presents little evidence of its former usefulness.

The Capt. Daniel Arnold House, built in 1714, was among the earliest of those left from the first dozen or so dwellings in the village group. While the original structure dates from that year; the present appearance of the building hardly indicates that fact. It has been added to, or rebuilt, at various times; and while some of the early work remains incorporated into the present house; the porch itself must date from one of the later reparations, probably about 1800.

This porch is representative of an unusual and individual local treatment of the entrance doorway feature, quite different from any other type that has been as well and thoroughly developed in this region of New England.

In Union Village itself may be found at least four examples of this distinctive and well marked type. All are very much alike; differing only in the handling of their detail. Each has a porch of ample depth, and rather wide spacing of the corner columns. Each has a plaster ceiling, of spacious arch segment section. In each case the house wall, inside the porch wall pilasters, is rusticated—in contrast to the remainder of the front wall surface, which is clapboarded after the usual and conventional fashion. In more than one case these porches now appear on dwellings that are themselves obviously of dates much older than the classical lines of these porches would seem to suggest.

That one which has been chosen for one of the measured drawings in this chapter is a case in point. The house itself dates back originally to 1714, being perhaps the third oldest now to be found in the existing group. The details of this particular example seem more *naïf* and interesting than any of the others. For that reason it has been chosen for detailed illustration. The same reasons suggest that it may be the earliest local example of the type; and that the others —or some of them—at any rate—may have later been modeled upon it. Certainly the more sophisticated moulding sections and treatment of the Allen doorway, along with the much smaller scale of the quoining, would suggest it as likely to have been of a later and more definitely classical school than the varied sections and ornament of this more sturdy and forceful example. Even the proportions of the paneled door itself are unusual; while the sectional projected caps that crown the two side architraves of the doorway are found in many other local examples, and the section through the keystone, along with its proportions and treatment, also recur elsewhere in the region; a similarity being traceable even in the key found in the other doorway detail, from the adjoining village of Slatersville, three miles away.

The original owners and builders of the Slatersville group were John and William Slater, who started the manufacture of cotton in the United States, beginning with a mill at Pawtucket, which is still standing— then shortly after establishing another upon the site of Slatersville. At that time, the problem confronting these mill builders was much the same as that faced by the manufacturers who built Bournedale and Port Sunlight. The location of the mill was more or less controlled by the availability of power and adjoining site—but it was necessary also to provide habitations for the factory help that were requisite to the success of the project. And so, in addition to the new mill, they built dwellings for their factory foremen and workers; and churches—and schools, too, for their children—along with the required stores, village center, hall and other necessities that were essential to secure the happiness and health of their employees, and make for the final success of the whole enterprise.

Slatersville itself—an unusual and charming mill village—contains the one individual and almost unique example of doorway that appears in the other measured drawing in this chapter. Nothing else of a similar design is now to be found either in these sections of northern Rhode Island, nor in those adjoin-

Porch and Doorway
WALTER ALLEN HOUSE – 1802 – UNION VILLAGE, RHODE ISLAND

ing them over the border of Massachusetts. The whole handling of the doorway is obviously local and rough in workmanship. The carving along the inner member of the architrave framing the entrance is roughly done, as though by a carpenter with only a gouge chisel for tool. The overwide pilasters are not in conformation with any classical proportions; just as their treatment—partly fluted; partly paneled, in height; and the final absurdity of cutting a glazed sash for a sidelight out of their very bosom, so to speak!—entirely defies the conventions, at nearly every point.

The rough and unusual sectioned capital and base mouldings are also unconventional, though well proportioned to their variation of customary precedent. But the final touch is the decoration contained in the upper panel of this pilaster—what would normally be regarded as the frieze of the composition. Here is located a crudely turned half-urn outline, again ornamented by grooved gouge chisel cuttings, to which have been appended unmistakable wings, with the feathering again suggested by the same instrument! Nothing else anything like this particular piece of detail can be recalled, except on some early headstones, where flying hourglasses or deaths heads, with similar crudely delineated pairs of wings, may sometimes be found. And these urns are here topped again with a sort of Spanish comb!

The cornice returns to something more akin to precedent—although overlight for its purpose here, in comparison with the wide and sturdily moulded wall-pilasters. But its wide projection, its delicately cut late mutules, and arched repeats with turned pendants (most of which vary widely in their turning, by the way!) along with its delicate crown mould, all suggest a date in the early 1800's for this portion of the design, at least. It is, of course, quite probable that the whole design is now the result of several fragmentary alterations or adaptations—which, nevertheless, does not in the least detract from its unusual architectural interest!

And the double house next door; between the one with this unique doorway and the village church, has a doorway of another—though more familiar—type, in this case one already widely shown from the region roundabout; and illustrated in other variations in the several examples from the Angell houses of Smithfield. (See Volume VI, Chapter 10.) It, too, possesses its own individual instance of local *naïveté!* Usually, this doorway with the semicircular toplight can only be placed in the small house, with its normal modest story height, be means of reducing the thickness of the floor joists over the hallway itself, or sometimes— when even that is not enough—by curving up the first floor hall plaster ceiling in a segment of an arch, fitted to meet the upper part of the rounded toplight frame. Sometimes this curve is carried out to the back of the wooden gallery board around the stair well; sometimes it is gradually worked down and out into the flat ceiling of the rest of the hallway. Occasionally—as in the

"Halfway" House doorway from Ashton; on page 181 in Volume VI, Chapter II—the space arched upon the exterior of the wall, is *not* opened through into the hallway and fitted with glass at all; but filled in, as was the case in that instance, by a flat wood panel, treated with a slat cut-pattern; or still another type of design, that usually simulates in form something suggesting the muntins of a possible glass toplight pattern.

In this house, the builder frankly accepted his established limitations, and shows enframed within the arch itself, a glass glazed sash that keeps below the set ceiling height at the same time that it cannot therefore conform to the height of the exterior arched portion of the design! This house has also been widened, by a wing at either side, into a "double house."

Of the houses shown, these are the only two from School Street, which is now the principal highway passing along eastward to Forestdale—another old mill village, established only a bare mile away; also having its own old mill cottages—although not grouped—nor so well and consistently maintaining any established type, as is the case at Slatersville. It is also lacking in the Green, so appealing at Slatersville.

The houses and doorways fronting upon the Green are attractive at first glance, because of an unusual success in grouping. They possess a considerable similarity of effect. Any closer study shows them to also contain, as markedly, differences in detail and treatment that give them the variety and individuality that we unconsciously require to avoid monotony. Some of them, individually, are more successful than others. All have been given covered living porches—placed usually at the sides or ends of the structures. Every architect knows how difficult it is to arrange such "modern necessities" so that they will not be a jarring note in the integrity of the Colonial house design!

Each reader may judge for himself, from the group photograph of the three houses shown in one view, as to the success of this venture, as it has been incorporated into the Slatersville group. Of course, in some examples the result has been more successful than in others. Perhaps, in the opinion of the writer, at least, the end porch added to the house with the vestibule (House "F" upon the sketch plan, page 147) appears to be about the best of them all.

With the entrance porches, or doorways, the same thing may also be said, though with more reservations. In the group of three houses, for instance, shown on page 147, the porch in the nearest seems among the least successful (again, of course, that is only the opinion of the writer!), while the house with the recessed doorway, with the suggestion of the slatted oval toplight, again fails in reproducing the best Colonial tradition! The entrance porch with pediment (House "E") would appear to be far more successful; while the projected vestibule, with the double pilastered front, belongs authentically in the proper tradition, even if it is not entirely the entrance that may have

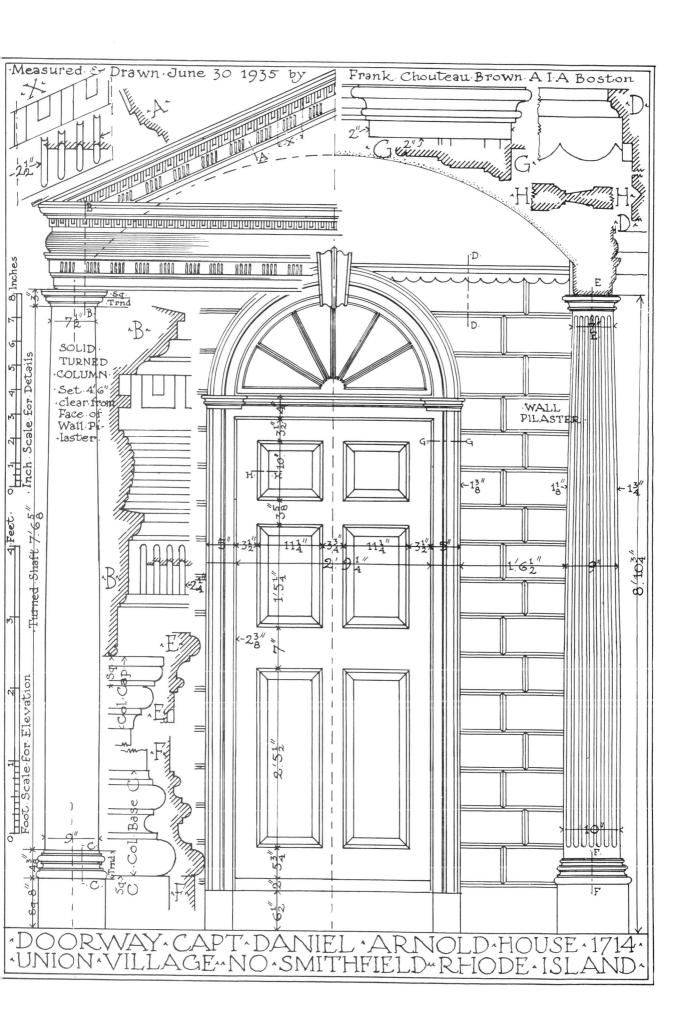

Measured & Drawn June 30 1935 by　　Frank Chouteau Brown A.I.A Boston

SOLID TURNED COLUMN Set 4'6" clear from Face of Wall Pilaster

WALL PILASTER

Foot. Scale for Elevation · Inch. Scale for Details

Turned Shaft 7'6⅝

Col. Sq. Cap

Col. Base

Sq. Trnd.

· DOORWAY · CAPT · DANIEL · ARNOLD · HOUSE · 1714 ·
· UNION · VILLAGE · NO · SMITHFIELD · RHODE · ISLAND ·

Porch and Doorway
CAPT. DANIEL ARNOLD HOUSE—1714—UNION VILLAGE, RHODE ISLAND

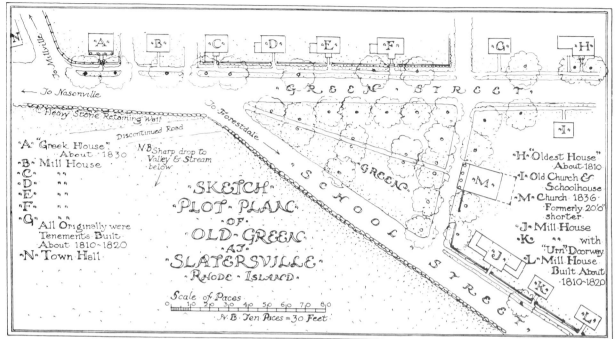

been originally upon the house as it was first erected!

As to Slatersville itself, at this late day there exists no one to prove that it may have been planned of intention. Possibly it comes within the same descriptive category as Topsy—who "jest growed!" The Church, which heads the Green, was built in 1836. The land contours being what they are, and the northern roadway—now known as Green Street—being the earlier in date; it would seem probable that

the diagonal path toward the Church may have gradually established itself—and then later, when the need for continuing School Street toward the west, to carry the increasing traffic coming from the south, became apparent—perhaps the existing heavy retaining walls were made or strengthened, and the present elms were planted, so as to make the Green more balanced.

Originally most of these houses were mill tenements, containing four families each; and therefore

VIEW OF GREEN STREET, SLATERSVILLE, SHOWING HOUSES "C" (left), "D," "E," AND "F"

Detail of Doorway
HOUSE "K", SCHOOL STREET, SLATERSVILLE, RHODE ISLAND

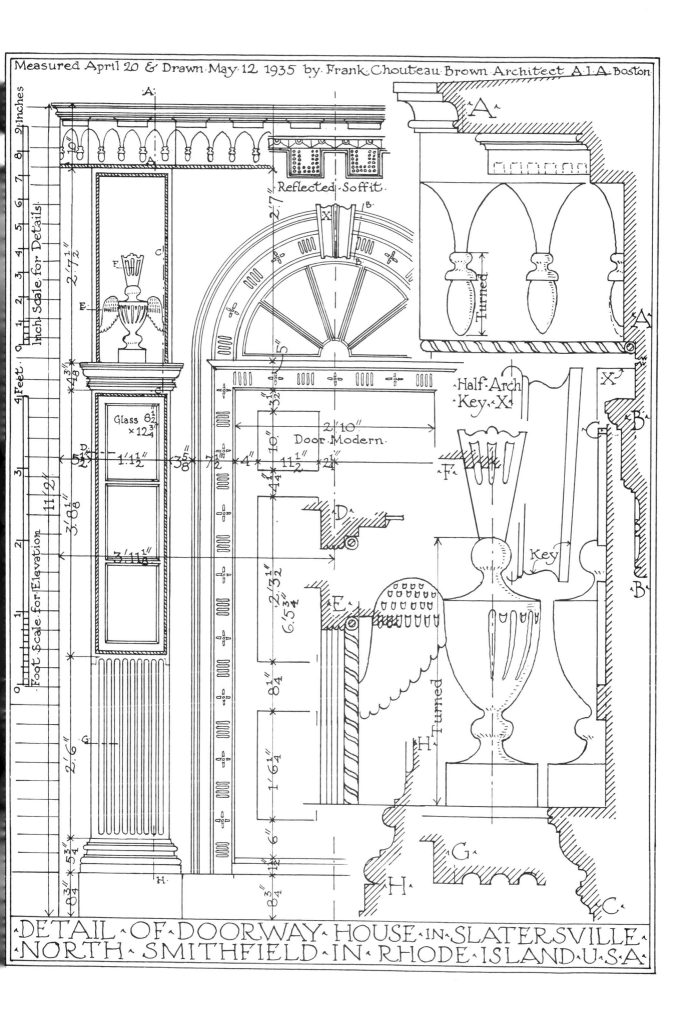

Measured April 20 & Drawn May 12 1935 by Frank Chouteau Brown Architect A.I.A. Boston

Reflected Soffit

Turned

Half Arch
Key X

Door Modern

Glass 6½" × 12¾"

Inch Scale for Details

Foot Scale for Elevation

Key

Turned

DETAIL OF DOORWAY HOUSE IN SLATERSVILLE
NORTH SMITHFIELD IN RHODE ISLAND U.S.A.

HOUSE "K", SCHOOL STREET, SLATERSVILLE, RHODE ISLAND

HOUSE "F", GREEN STREET, SLATERSVILLE, RHODE ISLAND

HOUSE "J", SCHOOL STREET, SLATERSVILLE, RHODE ISLAND

HOUSE "H" (PARSONAGE), GREEN STREET, SLATERSVILLE, RHODE ISLAND

they probably never possessed any interior finish of any great value. Within comparatively late years they have been improved and made over into single family dwellings; and in most cases the old doorways were retained, or were but slightly changed in appearance. The problem of changing levels of the site was met by the stone wall topped with a wooden fence, of various heights along these lot frontages; the informality of which contributes something to the charm of the whole.

Still further along Green Street, facing upon the side of the Church, is the house now used as the Rec-

into its present use as a two-family dwelling were not done in as good taste as the other changes in the group.

The Church appears in any general photograph of the group to far less advantage than it does in reality. While the distances are not great the camera lens makes its location seem very remote, in some cases — while in others the foliage serves to conceal the structure in large part. But seen from almost any point along the retaining wall that bounds the southern roadway upon the verge of the steep slope dropping down to the stream and mill in the valley below, these

HOUSE "D", GREEN STREET, SLATERSVILLE, RHODE ISLAND

tory; the doorway of which — here enframed in reeded pilasters — is representative of still another type, of which examples may be found in a number of villages scattered over a considerable area. The interior of this building retains three or more mantels, the old Dutch ovens, a winding staircase, and the old doors. Across the street from it stands the building that was originally used as a combined church and schoolhouse. The second Sunday school in the United States is believed to have been started in this structure. Unfortunately, the changes made in turning the building over

houses and their setting do much to prove that something was understood — however unconsciously — even at a date at least as early as 1800, of the possible beauty of combinations of house-grouping with open space and fences, and of shurb and tree planting, within the boundaries of old New England itself — and that precedents of mill village groups may be found indigenous to this country, that are at least as possible of latent charm and local color values as anything that can be garnered and adapted to the purpose from redigested precedents produced abroad.

Detail of Doorway
HOUSE "H", (PARSONAGE), GREEN STREET, SLATERSVILLE, RHODE ISLAND

Northeastern Rhode Island

Text by
Grover L. Jenks
Photographs by
Arthur C. Haskell
Originally published in 1935 as White Pine Monograph
Volume XXI, Number 3

Doorway
"HALFWAY" HOUSE AT SMITHFIELD, RHODE ISLAND

DWELLINGS IN NORTHEASTERN RHODE ISLAND AND THE SMITHFIELDS

SMITHFIELD (and North Smithfield) are traversed by three principal north and south thoroughfares, the Louisquisset, Douglas and Farnum "Pikes," of which the first named also passes through a part of Lincoln township. These old roadways have been enlarged and graded in recent years, but today the traveler, rolling easily along their well metalled surfaces, gains little idea of the heavier grades and slower routes, of which they were important existing elements at a far earlier time.

He will also get little idea of the real life of the localities through — but principally by — which he is passing; as most of the small villages lie off these main traveled routes, along with almost all the old farmhouses still left in this region. He will still be able to glimpse a few remnants of the old system of taverns that once flourished; but the old centers of industry, mills and houses, are mostly to be found on those steeper dirt roads that constantly cross and wind about the country, generally in an easterly or westerly direction, between these old pikes.

But that the old use of these north and south highways must have been considerable is evident from the great number of old inns and taverns that are still to be seen at many locations along their traveled margins; a large number despite the high mortality that seems to have attacked these old wayside houses of entertainment and hospitality — a mortality of which proof often remains in the very tangible form of high mounds of crumbling brickwork for the older, and the rugged and twisting outlines of still standing chimneys

for those more recently vanished. While lacking these direct proofs, another verdant witness may frequently be found, in the two clumps of old cedars — often of quite huge dimensions and height — that seem to have been the favorite and customary sentinels of the entrance gateways or doorstone boundaries of this region in early times; just as the spreading elms of Massachusetts and, farther north, the close groupings of overgrown lilacs may still be seen guarding the deserted home sites.

Smithfield itself still contains no less than three "Halfway" Houses in the district about ten miles above Providence, all once centers of activity and much frequented by the teaming confraternity during the period of a hundred to a hundred and fifty years or more ago. One of these, at a now quiet crossroads on the Farnum Pike, is shown on page 158, while a detail view of its principal entrance appears on the opposite page. Originally a smaller house, stopping just at the right of the main doorway, it was enlarged by adding the addition beyond this point, with a separate outside door to the barroom, and a larger room for dances and gatherings upon the floor above. Most of these interiors have lost whatever old finish they may have possessed; although it is seldom indeed that much pains was lavished upon the woodwork of the early inns of this district. Most attention was apparently paid to providing solid substantial construction, and ample fireplace and cooking facilities; along with the very important essential of commodious "stabling"; most of which latter construction has vanished altogether, except what has been found adaptable to be continued in use for the purposes of the simple farming.

As in other communities, these rolling acres were once possessed by large families; who spread from the original manors slowly over the sightly locations on the adjoining hillsides, as children grew up and married, and the parents provided them with domiciles nearby. This has been the common history of all New England communities; and it seems to have been particularly the case in this section of Rhode Island. But now

the proverbial "stone's throw" of each other, the older (Number One) has become a neglected tenement. Its eight-paneled doorway is surrounded by the more elaborated form of one of the most typical local doorway treatments.

To Angell House Number Two has befallen a better fate! Here an appreciative city family has moved in; and have gradually been uncovering and delighting in the quaint local treatments they have found in the architectural details of their new country home. While the woodwork around their doorway is of a

"HALFWAY" HOUSE ON FARNUM PIKE, SMITHFIELD, RHODE ISLAND

these old families have all gone; and their once beautifully furnished homes have either been taken over by a few city dwellers who have come out to this region to enjoy the healthful air and beautiful views, or they have fallen upon more evil days and passed into the possession of less appreciative residents, and degenerated to "country tenements" (than which no city variant can be more forlorn — or more teeming with a youthful population! — than these).

Contrasting examples of both these fates appear in the next two houses; known here only as Angell House Number One and Angell House Number Two! Originally, both were probably of nearly equal interest and both still convey the charm so expressive of their origin and period. As they now stand, quite within

simpler type of design, the proportions of the whole are more ample and hospitable compared to the narrow, higher composition of the neighbor house entrance design. The principal glory of this entrance is found in the beautiful metalwork of the round toplight, the details of which may be more clearly seen in the photographic detail shown on page 166, where it may be studied and contrasted with the similar toplight of the Steere House entrance, shown both there and in the detail drawing on page 167. The woodwork of the later doorway, taken in conjunction with the other two houses, shows the gradual evolution and simplification of the type, as it was worked upon by the carpenters local to the district. The earlier — Angell Number One — is of course the most "stilted"

Doorway

ANGELL HOUSE NUMBER ONE — c1780 — SMITHFIELD, RHODE ISLAND

in design; at the same time that it displays the most elaborate wood craftsmanship, but with a very simple wood toplight. The entablature is complete, and the pilaster has a separate and unusual decorated capital.

The Number Two House doorway shows the elimination of the conventional pilaster cap—and the architrave of the entablature continued of intention to perform both offices in the design. The grooved cutting around the door opening shows its close affinity with and relationship to the earlier doorway, where

justice. The ornaments employed are also rather frequently encountered in similar locations and use, in other houses not very far removed. It hardly seems possible that they could have been the product of any local artisan, no matter how skilled. Could it have been that it was at some time the custom to order these decorative adjuncts made from some city shop, in Providence or elsewhere, either to order, or from some "stock" catalogue, and have them made to dimension—to fit the wooden sash—which might perhaps even have been forwarded to the craftsman for

ANGELL HOUSE NUMBER ONE—c1780—SMITHFIELD, RHODE ISLAND

another type of carved grooved treatment, in the same position, is to be seen. And here the more elaborate leaded toplight design appears, introduced either originally into the doorway design, or possibly substituted for a simpler wooden pattern shortly after the house was built. In the Steere House doorway another experiment has been tried by the builder. He has now eliminated the entablature architrave and used instead the simplest of Doric moulded capital, to serve again two uses!

The great refinement and delicacy of the cast ornaments in these two arched glass lights can probably be realized, even if the drawing hardly does them

glazing? If so, it would explain a somewhat widespread use of similar arched lights, employing identical cast ornaments, differently assembled and combined, to be sure, but unquestionably cast from the same molds, and in a material susceptible of far more delicacy of modeling and perfection of detail than we are accustomed to find in the heavier cast leaden ornaments of the later "Colonial" doorlights of eastern Massachusetts, for instance!

The strips themselves are also not lead, but appear to be brass, weathered almost to a dark copper or gun metal tone, and of a very thin, narrow section with a raised bead on the top. See the drawing on page 167.

Doorway
ANGELL HOUSE NUMBER TWO — c1810 — SMITHFIELD, RHODE ISLAND

Wall Cupboard

Mantel

ANGELL HOUSE NUMBER TWO — c1810 — SMITHFIELD, RHODE ISLAND

JOSEPH MOWRY FARMHOUSE — c1701 — SMITHFIELD, RHODE ISLAND

Front Door
JOSEPH MOWRY FARMHOUSE — c1701 — SMITHFIELD, RHODE ISLAND

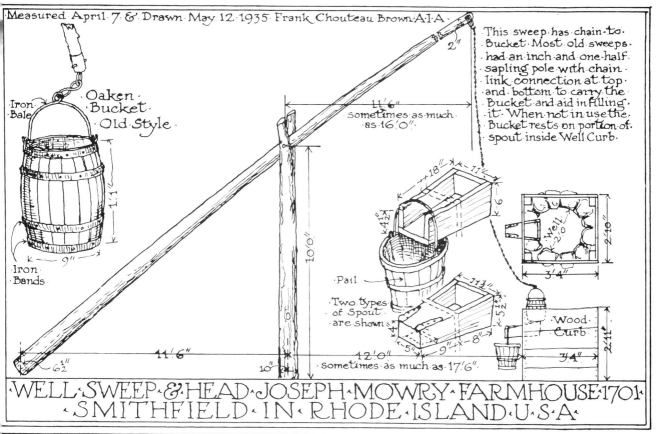

Iron Bale

Oaken Bucket Old Style

Iron Bands

This sweep has chain to Bucket Most old sweeps had an inch and one half sapling pole with chain link connection at top and bottom to carry the Bucket and aid in filling it. When not in use the Bucket rests on portion of spout inside Well Curb.

sometimes as much as 16'0"

11'6"

10'0"

Pail

Two types of Spout are shown

Well 2'0"

Wood Curb

11'6"

10" 2"

12'0" sometimes as much as 17'6"

3'4"

2'11"

WELL·SWEEP·&·HEAD·JOSEPH·MOWRY·FARMHOUSE·1701· ·SMITHFIELD·IN·RHODE·ISLAND·U·S·A·

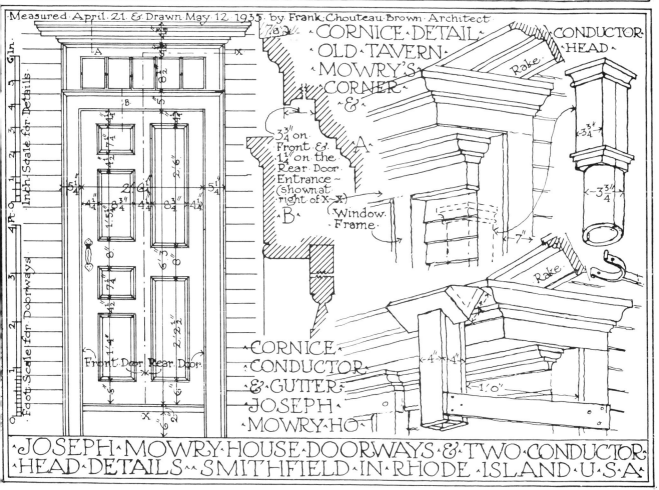

CORNICE·DETAIL· ·OLD·TAVERN· ·MOWRY'S· ·CORNER· ·&·

CONDUCTOR· ·HEAD·

Rake

3 3/4" on Front & 1 1/4" on the Rear Door Entrance (shown at right of X-X) ·B·

·A·

·Window· ·Frame·

Front Door Rear Door

·CORNICE· ·CONDUCTOR· ·&·GUTTER· ·JOSEPH· ·MOWRY·HO·

Rake

Inch Scale for Details   Foot Scale for Doorways

JOSEPH·MOWRY·HOUSE·DOORWAYS·&·TWO·CONDUCTOR· ·HEAD·DETAILS··SMITHFIELD·IN·RHODE·ISLAND·U·S·A·

Doorway Detail
ANGELL HOUSE NUMBER TWO, SMITHFIELD, RHODE ISLAND

Doorway Detail
STEERE HOMESTEAD, STILLWATER, RHODE ISLAND

Measured April 20. & Drawn May 3. 1935. by Frank Chouteau Brown. A.I.A. Boston.

Keystone

·Foot·Scale·for·Elevations·

·Inch·Scale·for·Details·

Lead·Z·Ornaments·X·in·Toplight·

Brackets·1¾″ wide on Face & 2½″ apart.

·DETAIL·OF·DOORWAY·STEERE·HOUSE·1825-30·
·STILLWATER·SMITHFIELD·IN·RHODE·ISLAND·

The interior of the second Angell House has a very delicately detailed stairway, and some very charming wood ornament and moulding in the principal downstairs room, with the use of some unusual—or, at least, unconventional—mouldings. In the room cornice, for instance, is to be seen a mould made up of continuous guttae; and an attractive and unusual treatment is shown in the dado cap, as well. The wall cupboard is out of the usual in the arrangement both of its doors, and the moulding and pilaster enframement; treatments that are very nearly echoed at the mantel;

ried out and around this short curtain wall, returning at each end, and coming in at the back of this flying false-wall again to the side of the projecting breast of the chimney.

The Joseph Mowry House is in another part of the township, quite near the solitary building that is its post office, and appears to mark its theoretical—and entirely vacant!—center; rather confusing to the tourist, hurrying along the thoroughfare, awaiting arrival at the town and then suddenly awaking to find himself some miles beyond the spot marked

STEERE HOUSE—1825–1830—STILLWATER, SMITHFIELD, RHODE ISLAND

where, with that naiveté that is occasionally found in historical designing, the pilasters do not set under the entablatures they support, moulding facures are projected beyond, or withdrawn inside, those relations they customarily bear to their neighbor elements. This whole design was motivated by the desire to secure as wide a fire opening as was possible in a comparatively restricted chimney, narrowed by being contained between two window openings. The result was secured in the masonry; and then the mantel was also widened by frankly extending the pilaster face treatment, out beyond the sides of the breast, in a thin wooden projection, that allowed of the shelf mouldings being car-

"Smithfield" upon his map, and being quite unable to remember passing any buildings, even a crossroads, sufficient to mark the "center"! Taken along with the fact that all the maps of rural Rhode Island—even the highway maps issued by the state—are entirely "screwy" both as to directions, town locations, and even the numbering of the highways; that no names are placed at intersections or street crossings over large areas of the state; and that none of the roadways shown even approximate the directions and changes of angles actually attained upon the terrain; this lack of landmarks makes touring within certain sections of this area even today something closely approaching all the uncertainties and thrills of real adventure! But to return and try and find the Mowry House again! It was first glimpsed flung far out upon a jutting hillside, with no apparent means of approach. By sharp eyesight, good luck and the exercise of considerable acumen, deduction, and prestidigitation, a practicable means was finally discovered, and the quite rural and charmingly informal arrangement shown in the picture was disclosed. The wellsweep had been

pears from the sketch of the cornice, where its relation to the window frames is also indicated, and particularly the beautiful wooden conductor, worked from two pieces of stock, and round below the head, is drawn out, as well as the type of iron holder—restored from a fragment found on the ground below. A portion of the "V" shaped gutter, similar to that on the Joseph Mowry House shown below it, was also still lying upon the ground. As indicated, it was

LATHAM COTTAGE—c1720—NEAR MOWRY'S CORNER, SMITHFIELD, RHODE ISLAND

partly modernized and rebuilt, but the older part of the house, that nearest the road, dated from 1701, with one of the simplest and best proportioned doorways (the one at the rear containing an old four-panel door—rather rarely encountered; and well worth studying for contrast with the modern "stock" travesties of the same type of design!).

Not far above Stillwater, where the Steere House stands on the hilltop above the old millsite and dam, that partly floods the valley below, is the old crossroads known as Mowry's Corner. Here still stands the old tavern that gave the crossing its name. This older house has considerable charm of detail, as ap-

made from old boards, ¾" thick, and 4" wide.

Not far away from the "Corner" is the old Latham Cottage, as delightful a composition of gambrel roof slopes as may be found in the old "Plantations."

Upon a rolling open hillside, not far above the Joseph Mowry Farmhouse stands the Old Appleby House, now much modernized to serve its summer pose of housing a large family. The porch at the corner—from which the best view and the coolest breeze may be found!—was formerly the old kitchen ell, and at the rear a new wing has been built; but the old door is still found in its unusual location, as part of the composition of the end gable.

OLD APPLEBY HOUSE, SMITHFIELD, RHODE ISLAND

The Blackstone River Valley

Text by
Frank Chouteau Brown
Photographs by
Arthur C. Haskell
Originally published in 1935 as White Pine Monograph
Volume XXI, Number 2

Doorway
FISK HOUSE, CUMBERLAND HILL, RHODE ISLAND

RHODE ISLAND HOUSES ALONG THE
BLACKSTONE RIVER VALLEY

AMONG the several famous people identified with the early history of Rhode Island; and especially with the rather little known history of that section located in its northeastern corner, are Samuel Newman and William Blackstone—or Blaxton, as he himself preferred to spell his name.

About the latter individual have clustered many legends; although most of those best known are told in connection with his occupancy of the land that is now comprised in the downtown business section of Boston; or with the area of its famous Boston Common. From any knowledge of these tales, it would appear that William Blackstone must have been both an interesting and unusual man; albeit very likely somewhat independent in his thought and perhaps eccentric in his manners, and possibly a better friend if living somewhat removed than when a next-door neighbor—or even as a "neighbor," living at the somewhat remote distances that were then the custom, rather than the exception, in this new land!

It is at any rate quite certain that, before the advent of Governor Winthrop and his companions, in 1630, upon the shores of Massachusetts Bay, Blackstone was a still earlier settler upon the eminence now known as Beacon Hill, in what was the peninsula then called Shawmut, meaning a spring of water. He was probably quite justly entitled to be called the "first white settler" of the land he occupied, within the area of the now populous and important city of Boston, in the Commonwealth of Massachusetts. Exactly how or when he arrived there is not quite so certain. Yet of the several theories that have been advanced, not the least improbable is the suggestion that he may have been among the group of early colonists that Robert Gorges, son of the better known Ferdinando Gorges (a well known English gentleman, despite his Spanish-sounding name, generally more popularly connected with certain early settlements in the region of the Kennebecs, now in the state of Maine), established at Weymouth, on Massachusetts Bay, under a patent issued in 1623.

In England, Mr. Blackstone had been born in 1595; had become a clergyman of the Established Church; and a graduate of Emanuel College at Cambridge, with the degree of A.B. in 1617.

And, inasmuch as he had removed from his pleasant home in England because of the increasing presence of his adjoining "neighbors," it may quite well have been that, in the wider and more open spaces of the new environment, he may have found a more perfect seclusion for his contemplation of the beauties of nature and the study of his dearly beloved library of "bookes," in the comparatively isolated and rarified heights of the "trimontaine" upon the then narrow tip of the natural peninsula that is now outspread into the city of Boston; but was then only connected with the mainland by the narrow isthmus whose original meanderings are still indicated by the windings of Washington Street, as it extends from downtown Boston to the heights of Roxbury.

At any rate, there he was, living in a small wooden hut—within the area now bounded by Beacon, Wal-

Doorway

ISRAEL ARNOLD HOUSE — 1790 — LINCOLN, RHODE ISLAND

Doorway

ELEAZER ARNOLD HOUSE, LINCOLN, RHODE ISLAND

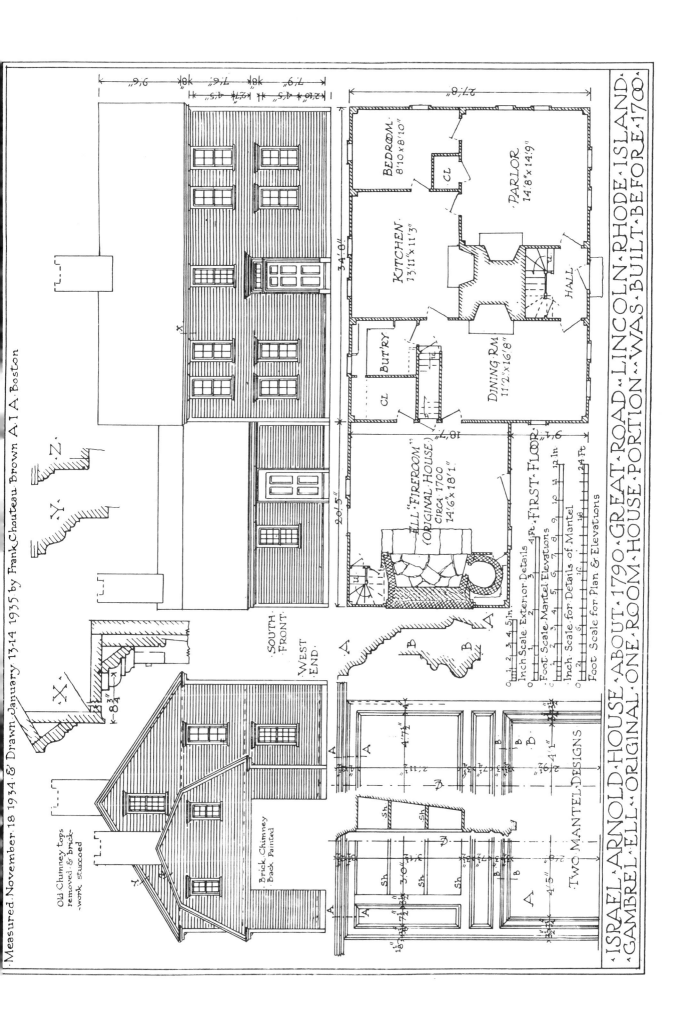

Measured November 18 1934 & Drawn January 13·14 1935 by Frank Chouteau Brown A·I·A·Boston

Old Chimney tops removed·& brick -work stuccoed

·X·

·Y· ·Z·

·SOUTH· ·FRONT·

·WEST· ·END·

Brick Chimney Back Painted

K-8'3/4"-

BEDROOM· 8'10"x8'10"

KITCHEN· 13'11"x 11'3"

CL

CL

BUT'RY

PARLOR· 14'8"x 14'9"

HALL·

DINING·RM· 11'2"x16'8"

ELL·"FIREROOM" (ORIGINAL·HOUSE) CIRCA 1700 14'6"x 18'1"

27'8"

34'0"

·FIRST·FLOOR·

A

A

B

B

B

B

A

A

A

A

Sh

Sh

Sh

Sh

B

B

B

B

·TWO·MANTEL·DESIGNS·

0 1 2 3 4·5·In. Inch Scale Exterior Details
1 2 3 4 Ft.
0 1 2 3 4 5 6 In. Foot Scale Mantel Elevations
0 1 2 3 4 5 6 7 8 9 10 11 12 In. Inch Scale for Details of Mantel
0 4 8 12 16 20 24 Ft. Foot Scale for Plan & Elevations

·ISRAEL·ARNOLD·HOUSE·ABOUT·1790·GREAT·ROAD·LINCOLN·RHODE·ISLAND· ·GAMBREL·ELL·ORIGINAL·ONE·ROOM·HOUSE·PORTION·WAS·BUILT·BEFORE·1700·

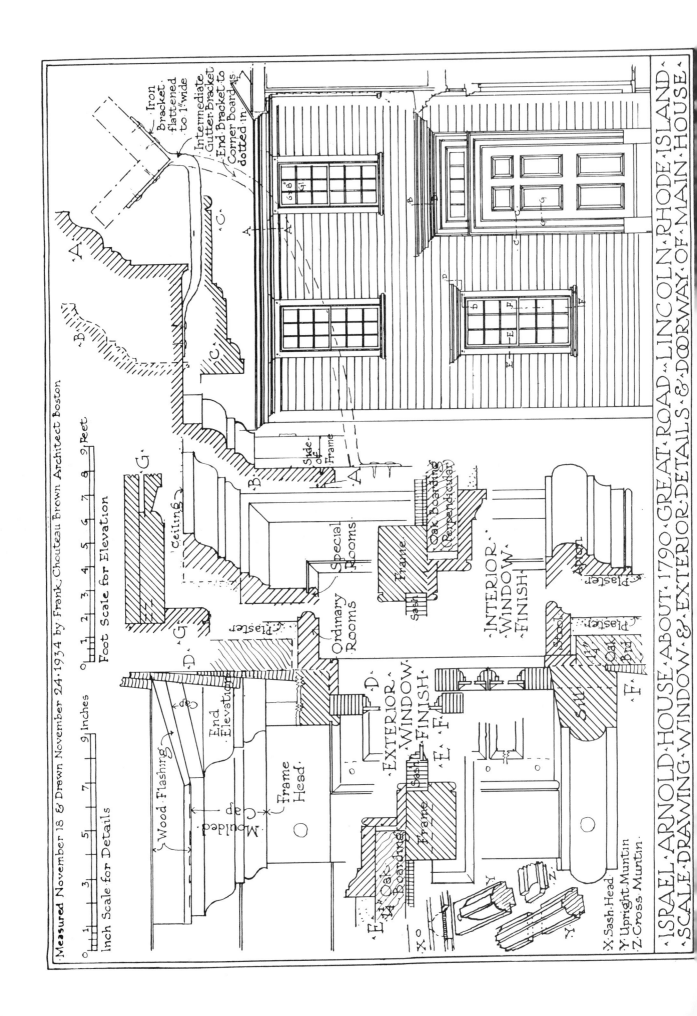

ISRAEL·ARNOLD·HOUSE·ABOUT·1790·GREAT·ROAD·LINCOLN·RHODE·ISLAND·
·SCALE·DRAWING·WINDOW·&·EXTERIOR·DETAILS·&·DOORWAY·OF·MAIN·HOUSE·

Measured November 18 & Drawn November 24·1934 by Frank·Chouteau Brown Architect Boston

0 1 3 5 7 9 Inches
Inch Scale for Details

0 1 2 3 4 5 6 7 8 9 Feet
Foot Scale for Elevation

Iron Bracket flattened to 1" wide

Intermediate Gutter Bracket. End Bracket to Corner Board as dotted in.

·A·

·B·

·C·

·G·

·G·

·D·

Ceiling

Plaster

·G·

Ordinary Rooms

Special Rooms

Frame

Sash

Oak Boarding (Perpendicular)

·INTERIOR·
·WINDOW·
·FINISH·

Plaster

Side of Frame

·B·

·A·

6'8"

·A·

·F·

·E·

·E·

·F·

·C·

·C·

·D·

·G·

·G·

End Elevation

Wood Flashing

Moulded Cap

Frame Head

·1" Oak Boarding

Frame

Sash

·EXTERIOR·
·WINDOW·
·FINISH·
·E·   ·F·

·D·

Sill

1" Oak Bd

Plaster

·F·

X·Sash·Head·

Y·

Z·

X·

Y·

X: Sash Head.
Y: Upright Muntin.
Z: Cross Muntin.

SPAULDING HOUSE, LINCOLN, RHODE ISLAND

nut, and Spruce streets—beside a clear and sparkling spring, on the slopes of the "Trimount" at Shawmut—when, in 1630, Winthrop and his companions, having removed from Salem (then Naumkeag) to another peninsula, upon the other side of the Charles River, also upon Boston Harbor; finding the water unpleasant and malignant, were glad to accept the Reverend Blackstone's invitation to cross to his side of the Charles, and settle upon the land remaining outside his farmstead, on what was then often referred to as Blackstone's Neck or Blackstone Point.

But, as had happened before in his experience, he soon began to feel unduly crowded by his new neighbors; whose increasing numbers may well have begun to interfere with his desire for quiet and solitude; while it is also quite as likely that he may have become somewhat dissatisfied with their religious intolerance—religion being a matter upon which he was well known as having very decided and somewhat individual views of his own! At any rate, by 1663 it was apparent that causes of dissatisfaction had arisen; and despite the fact that it was in that year that they set off for his exclusive ownership "fifty acres of land near his house," he soon found that he could not continue to endure their crowding numbers!

It was this land, partly used by him at that time as an "orchard" (a word probably then employed in its old English sense, rather than in its narrower modern meaning) and pasture, that has now come down—in large part—to the inhabitants of Boston as their Boston Common. It was first used, after Blackstone's departure in 1635, both as a cow pasture and as the town Training Field; while a small part of the original area was set apart as certain building sites—such as a portion east of the present Park Street, and south of its present Tremont Street boundary.

After another year of "neighborly existence," William Blackstone finally agreed to dispose of all his property rights in the peninsula to the inhabitants of Boston, on the payment by each and every householder, of at least six shillings (and some of them paid him a considerable amount more!).

It was probably in the following spring that he arose and, packing up his books, taking a considerable number of his favorite apples as seedlings, and buying himself a "stock of cowes," he started out in his "Canonical coate," over the then untraveled wilderness to the south, toward the headwaters of Narragansett Bay, to find for himself a new home, at some point where he could enjoy that "solitude," of which he had so long been in search, in a less known and populous portion of the country. This was more than a year before his friend Roger Williams was forced to fly from Salem, in the dead of winter; but Blackstone's pilgrimage, encumbered by his unusually weighty and bulky possessions, must have been a more leisurely and

pleasant journey; and it may have been on this very occasion that the legend of his riding his white bull or cow was evolved. Livestock—of any kind—were then rare, and horses very hard to obtain, so it was then the very general custom to make use of the slower but stronger cow as a beast of burden, much in demand where oxen or horses were not to be had.

It was so that he removed to a new home on the eastern bank of the Pawtucket—now the Blackstone—River; then a part of Plymouth Territory, or the Old Colony; as it was contained within the boundaries of Massachusetts, up to 1747; when Cumberland was at last set off to Rhode Island. The site of his dwelling has been very definitely established, from the old land records and other documents. As indication of his nature and desires, he named his new home Study Hall, and built it only a few rods from the banks of the Pawtucket River, at the foot of a hill, near a brook called Abbott's Run, in what is known as the Attleboro Gore, about three miles above the city of Pawtucket, in the present town of Lonsdale.

This was when William Blackstone was thirty-nine years old, and almost two years before Roger Williams left Salem to first settle in Seekonk, in 1636, from which he soon removed across the river to Providence. Yet even here Blackstone could not long maintain that complete isolation that he so much desired; for it appears from a record of a meeting held in December, 1650, that one of the earliest of still existing roads passed nearby his home. The vote, as inscribed upon the town records, reads "—to have a convenient way, 4 rods wide, to be made by Edward Smith, to be for the town's use, or any that shall have occasion to pass from town to Providence, or to Mr. Blackstone's." And the road laid out at that time still crosses the Blackstone River, at the old Wading Place, opposite Study Hall, and is now known as the Mendon Road. It bounded Blackstone's Study Hall on the east and northeast. But while the roadway remains, Study Hall itself has long disappeared, even some of the eminence having been partly leveled to provide room for a busy cotton mill on the banks of the river (the Hope Mill) near which is a marker, erected in 1889, and located only a few yards from Blackstone's grave and in line with it, the exact site being now under a nearby portion of the mill buildings.

Blackstone did not die until May 26, 1675; when he was eighty years old; and it would appear that in his later years he became less of a recluse than had been his former reputation. He frequently visited his friend, Roger Williams, who had come to live only about six miles from him; as well as another man well known in the early annals of Rhode Island, Richard Smith, at his fine old mansion at Wickford. On these visits it was Blackstone's custom to carry with him apples from his flourishing orchards (some of the trees

MOWRY SMITH HOUSE, LINCOLN, RHODE ISLAND

Doorway
MOWRY SMITH HOUSE AT LINCOLN, RHODE ISLAND

Doorway

"HALFWAY" HOUSE AT ASHTON, RHODE ISLAND

he set out were living 140 years after!) to give to the children he knew along the roads, thus probably establishing the many excellent fruit trees for which the township of Cumberland and Lincoln are still famous!

And by this somewhat devious road, have we come again into the old township of Lincoln, for Study Hall and Lonsdale are within only a mile or two of the group of Arnold houses, which stand only a little nearer to Saylesville than to Lonsdale, and about an equal distance from Central Falls, just north of the city of Pawtucket, with which place the story of the

both to the east and the west, run the old roads and modern highways, built up to bear its traffic and output; and still preserving access to many of the older settlements and isolated houses that have survived.

And backing them again, on the sloping uplands and hillsides of Cumberland and Lincoln townships, and along the less used dirt roads crossing the main highways, from east to west, may be found the simple, reserved dwellings and farmsteads, bringing down to our day their atmosphere of the middle and late eighteenth century life, as they have preserved its

"HALFWAY" HOUSE, ASHTON, RHODE ISLAND

Reverend Samuel Newman is more closely connected, and so it may well be set aside to await the description of the origins of that township.

Meanwhile, it is this Blackstone River Valley, once for so long a time the natural boundary between the Commonwealth of Massachusetts and the Providence Plantations in Rhode Island, that commands our attention. A valley that, once quiet and secluded, is now filled with close set and crowded mill buildings for its entire length, from Massachusetts to the bay. And, paralleling its steep rising banks, upon the higher land

flavor over the long years that have elapsed between.

Besides the remaining examples showing the early type of "one-room house" that came into existence in Rhode Island during the seventeenth century; Lincoln township and its immediately adjoining areas still preserves a number of interesting dwellings of the later period, particularly those built during the middle and last part of the eighteenth century. One of the most unusual and picturesque examples is the Captain John Jenks House, which is shown on page 219 of Volume VI, Chapter 13. Captain Jenks was of the fourth generation of the founders of Pawtucket, and the east end of the structure, built in 1770, was the workshop, which he left to serve in the Revolutionary War. The west end, with its unusual gambrel resting upon the ground, dates from 1800 and was used as the first schoolhouse in that region.

Of the group of Arnold houses shown in that same chapter, the Israel Arnold dwelling now stands with a newer portion, built some time before 1790, attached to the original one-room structure, which dates from about 1700. In many ways this newer part is typical,

While the exterior discloses as well the harmonious details of eaves, windows, and doorways; and makes the relation between the two portions much more definite and understandable, for those who may desire to make a special study of the character of this house; which, in its location, seems to possess a dignity and individuality all its own.

The group of Arnold houses that is shown in Chapter 13 located just beyond the Quaker Meeting House, a very short distance from Smithfield Avenue, in that part of the town of Lincoln that

MATHURIN BALLOU HOUSE, SAYLESVILLE, RHODE ISLAND

in its finish, as well as its plan, of other houses in the vicinity dating from about the same time. This is especially true of some of the interior details such as the mantels and window trim. The same sections and treatment of the inside trim may be found in houses in Cumberland and Attleboro; in Smithfield, Gloucester, and Cranston. And for that reason it has been chosen to serve as the subject of the measured drawing in this chapter. It thus supplements the more unusual and earlier treatments of the "stone chimney houses" to which Chapter 13 is more fully devoted.

is nearest to North Providence, known as Saylesville. The Mathurin Ballou House, shown in this chapter, is in the same settlement; and may be taken as characteristic of the simplest type of country dwelling of the eighteenth century still to be found in that region. Its simplicity extends even to the extreme of giving the principal entrance doorway no more embellishment than the practical wood lintel that in shape suggests derivation from the flat masonry or brick arch found in many Colonial structures. As a matter of fact, this cap is a very practical solution of the flashing problem, and is found in use over a large area in this portion of New England. It is made from a heavy piece of timber—often of hard wood—overhanging the delicately moulded enframement of the opening below, and placed against the face of the frame boarding. The top is sloped and the grain runs horizontally; so that, combined with the eight to ten inches height of the member, it is about as fine a weather protection as could be effected from locally available material at that time. The irregular spacing of the windows is also usual in these districts, where

capped with the same wood "lintel" pattern; but the doorway is one of the favorite and more elaborate designs, which will be found upon a number of other dwellings, all over this northeastern Rhode Island section. It shows the arch contained within an open pediment; and the classical details of the pilastered order are here worked out with a care and harmony evidencing both knowledge and skill on the part of the designer or builder. The pilaster is boldly projected, the Renaissance Doric detail of triglyph and capital well worked out; but the cornice is of a more elabo-

ALDRICH HOUSE, LIMEROCK, RHODE ISLAND

apparently their arrangement was determined exclusively by considerations of practical use on the interior and in the plan.

The main highway turns to the right just beyond Saylesville, toward Lonsdale and the crossing of the Blackstone River at the location of William Blackstone's old dwelling of Study Hall. The traveler is now on the old Mendon Road, which runs along the higher land and parallels the river along its eastern side. "Halfway" House at Ashton, is a bit more sophisticated solution of the local dwelling design. The house is deeper and more pretentious, the windows are

rate type, avoiding the heavy overhang and soffit treatment of the regular Roman precedent, and substituting a heavy running dentil-fret of a carefully adapted scale instead. This example is among the most successful of this particular type, despite the unfortunate emphasis by means of the strongly contrasted two-color scheme, that has been arbitrarily applied over its detail and which considerably obscures its architectural merits.

This doorway is one of several that also display the substitution of an applied pattern over a plain wooden face within the arched head of the nominal opening—

in this case employing an unusual heart-shaped motif that has been very ingeniously adapted to meet the outlines of the arched design. In the several examples of this treatment seen, it was hardly obvious that it had been later substituted for any earlier glass toplight; but rather, as in this particular example, it seemed to have been the original method employed by the builder to carry out his design, and suggest its desired treatment, even if the use of glass was prevented by the toplight arch extending up above the location of the second floor in the dwelling's façade.

Farther to the north, along this same Mendon Road, is Cumberland Hill; a small settlement with several old dwellings, one of stone, that are in no case of exceptional architectural merit, despite their local interest. Here the old Fisk House may be taken as fairly representative of another local variant of the favorite dwelling type. Again the structure is a large one, even deeper in plan than the last example, as a matter of fact—while the windows have the "lintel" treatment, used under the cornice across the front (where, as a matter of fact, this protection is hardly needed and therefore rather rarely found). The first story and end windows have a much thinner wood window head flashing, such as is more often met with over a wider New England area. The entrance is again typical—but this time of another favorite local design. Again the details are very closely derived from Classical Roman precedent, employing the regular Renaissance bracket in the entablature, with a fat curved section to the frieze. The necking of the capital is rather too narrow—a fault often found in similar designs in this vicinity, by the way—and the pilaster bases are here intact; the pilasters themselves being of more modest and conventional projection. The door suffers from the substitution of glass in two of its former eight panels.

Undoubtedly the tower on this house would be challenged as original by any stranger visiting the locality; but the local claim to its authenticity is generally voiced. The example here shown is said to have been formerly of two more stories high; and it is also claimed that there were originally towers upon at least two other old houses nearby, that have now been taken down; the legend being that they were originally used as outlooks for the French troop outposts, at the time when they were in garrison in this part of Rhode Island!

Another example of this same house design type appears in the Mowry Smith House, where the "lintel" window cap again is used. In this place the end doorway was originally near the front corner of the house; where the clapboards are obviously new, even in the photograph; and where may still be seen the large doorstone of the old entranceway. The front door design is a less conventional expression of the Fisk House type, with a glass toplight introduced above the door

frame architrave, and the capital necking extended to correspond with it in height! A bit of local naïveté obviously to be attributed to the carpenter-builder—who was probably copying some imperfectly remembered doorway. The Mowry Smith House is located in a remote portion of the township, upon a road that shortly after passing this farmhouse goes on to lose itself in a rocky, barren hill country.

One of the most picturesque and beautiful portions of Lincoln township is in that section known as Limerock. Limerock lies to the east of the Louisquisset Pike, the principal thoroughfare from Providence to Worcester and Woonsocket, between that roadway and the Blackstone River.

Shortly after leaving Lonsdale, this road passes the old Spaulding House, a rather later and more elaborate dwelling, of extra length—even after ignoring the more palpably modern addition at its southern end. The rear of the house overlooks a meadow extending to the Blackstone River, and it lies in a pleasantly quiet and retired location, that should make it an ideal summer retreat for some harried business man. Unfortunately the house has suffered much, both from neglect and "modernization," at the hands of several owners. The window caps are moulded, and the doorway is similar to the last two houses mentioned, although the door has again had glass substituted for some of its original wood panels, and has been given a pair of blind doors that somewhat conceal its pilaster framing.

To anyone interested in the old industries of the region, by turning off the river road in front of this house and climbing a winding dirt roadway for a short three-quarters mile, he will be rewarded by coming out upon a hilltop where the road passes between a deep cut quarry at his left and huge stacks of cordwood and a group of lime kilns at his right. Here he may see lime still being wood-burned after the old tried-and-true fashion—now almost extinct!

By continuing along this winding rock-and-cedar-bounded road, the traveler may turn to the left and return toward Providence by the Arnold houses; or, by turning north, he will soon come to the cluster of old structures making up the ancient village of Limerock. Here may be found the old Mowry Tavern, a portion dating back to 1684; and a brick Masonic Lodge building—while climbing up to a row of more modern houses overlooking the valley—and passing by another example of stone chimney-end house—may be found a group of newer dwellings, including one charmingly planned and scaled house with an unusual Greek feeling. Or, turning about and going in the opposite direction, toward the west, one will pass the Aldrich House—again of the usual local type, but with pilasters at the doorway that have omitted the necking and necking moulding altogether.

Doorway
ALDRICH HOUSE, LIMEROCK, RHODE ISLAND

Rhode Island Mill Towns

Text by
A. N. Fowler
Photographs by
Arthur C. Haskell
Originally published in 1936 as White Pine Monograph
Volume XXII, Number 2

HOUSE AT FISKEVILLE, RHODE ISLAND

RHODE ISLAND MILL TOWNS

IN the early days it was necessary to weave all cloth by hand, in the colonies as well as in England. The only mechanical aid employed being small frames used to hold the material in position. In 1767 James Hargreaves invented in England the "spinning jenney," which made it possible to spin eight threads at once instead of the single one that was all that could be done previously on a spindle. Roller spinning was next perfected by Richard Arkwright, and all the preliminary processes of cotton manufacture were for the first time brought within one building. This was the start of the English factory system.

In 1779 Samuel Crompton of Bolton combined the spinning jenney of Hargreaves, with the water frame of Arkwright, into the "spinning-mule." All these improvements had been made within a small district in England; and the government prohibited the export of any cotton machinery — as well as of any plans, drawings or models, in an effort to restrict the center of the world cotton industry within Great Britain.

In 1786, two Scotsmen, Alexander and Robert Barr, in the employ of Mr. Orr of East Bridgewater, Massachusetts, made the first machines for the carding, roving and spinning of cotton in this country — and the state legislature granted £200 to encourage and further that work. The next year the Beverly Company, of Beverly, Massachusetts, spent £4000 and in 1790 were given a grant of £1000 from the legislature, and started in the manufacture of cotton goods with very imperfect machinery.

In Providence a company was formed to make "homespun" cloths in 1788, on machinery made from drawings of English models, and plans from Orr and the Beverly Company — but carding and roving were still very imperfectly done by hand labor, and the spinning frame — carrying thirty-two spindles — was little better than the common jenney, turned by a hand crank. This machinery was sold to Moses Brown of Providence, who — with William Almy — had several "hand jennies" installed in private houses in Providence, making yarn for the weft of mixed linen and cotton stock.

Samuel Slater, born in Belper (Derbyshire), England, June 9, 1768, learned to spin cotton with Jedidiah Strutt, who, in association with Sir Richard Arkwright, was running a mill at Milford, England; where Slater worked for about eight years. He became a good machinist, and after the term of his apprenticeship had expired, he happened to see a Philadelphia paper in which a reward was offered by some society, for a device to make cotton rollers. He sailed to America on September 13, 1789, and after a voyage of sixty-six days arrived in New York and went to work for a manufacturing company in that city; but their machinery was imperfect, and their water power transmission unsatisfactory. While there, he heard from a captain of a sailing packet, of Mr. Moses Brown of Providence, being interested in cotton making; and wrote to offer his services, and in January of 1790 he had arranged to go to Almy & Brown in Pawtucket.

He started work January 18, and by December 20 he had three cards drawing and roving, and seventy-two spindles worked by an old fulling mill waterwheel; and at the end of twenty months they had several thousand pounds of yarn on hand. Early in 1793, Almy, Brown & Slater built a small factory in Pawtucket (since known as the Old Factory) and opened it on July 12, Slater having built new machinery, on English models, entirely from memory.

In 1798, Slater joined with Ozial Wilkinson, whose daughter he had married, along with two other brothers-in-law, Timothy Green and William Williamson, in building a second mill, on the east side of the Pawtucket River, as Samuel Slater & Co. and superintended the two mills, being paid $1.50 the day by each; while he soon became interested in other mills situated in other Rhode Island and Massachusetts villages nearby along the Blackstone River.

up as a sort of museum, in which can now be seen many of the early milling experiments. The second mill used in the making of cotton in that state is the Lippett Mill, built in 1809 near the northwestern corner of the township of West Warwick, about in the geographical center of the many little groups of old mill villages along the Pawtucket River, from which the majority of the cottages shown in this chapter have been taken.

This structure appears to be characteristic of most of the early mills in that vicinity. They were usually built of stone, three or four stories high, with the long roof broken by a sort of continuous dormer or monitor, sometimes continuing out to the very end walls of the

COTTAGES AT WEST WARWICK, RHODE ISLAND

Originally, as in England, these mills only manufactured the yarn, the weaving still being done in private houses—but the power loom, invented by the Rev. Edmund Cartwright in 1785, gradually came into use—and in 1813, at Waltham, Massachusetts, was built the first mill in the world, in which all the processes of making cotton cloth were carried on under one roof!

The first cotton mill in Rhode Island is still to be seen at Pawtucket, only a few miles up the Blackstone River from Providence. This is the mill where Samuel Slater, aided by money provided by Moses Brown of that latter city, made his first cotton weaving machines after the English model. The building has been fitted

building, and sometimes stopping from six to ten feet back from the end gable. While most of the old mill buildings in this vicinity have either entirely disappeared, or their sturdy walls have been built into later extensions, adding more stories to their height or increasing their length, until all semblance of the old building has disappeared; this one early example has happened to be preserved, with substantially little exterior change, so that it can still give us today an excellent picture of this original type. One other mill, the Jackson, may also be found upon the river bank, a few miles away. The Jackson mill was built in 1824, and from the river end it still shows the original outline, but upon the end toward the street, it has been

LIPPETT MILL — 1809 — WEST WARWICK, RHODE ISLAND

INTERLARKEN MILLS COTTAGE, HARRIS, RHODE ISLAND

given a later extension that entirely conceals the older part of the structure.

Most of the cottages that were originally grouped about the Lippett Mill have now disappeared, or been hopelessly "modernized" by ugly changes and additions—but the pair of tenements picturesquely grouped with the single tree remaining from the old row along the village street, are all that now preserve the character of the old group. They date from about the same year as the mill structure. Nearby are also several larger tenements, each built to contain eight families; but the renewal of sash, additions of dormers, and destruction of the old trees, leaves little but their most prosaic outlines now to be seen.

From the similarity of the old mill buildings, as well as the repetition—in village after village—of smaller cottages of precisely the same type; it would appear that most of these developments were probably constructed by the same builders, if not for the same company. Therefore it would seem that the older

among these cottages date from between 1809 and 1812. Certainly those built in this period are among the nicest in proportion and detail. Another group, using almost the same plans, and but slightly different in detail, were probably constructed between about 1815 and 1820. Their appearance is much the same, and their mouldings but slightly different. And then another lot appears to have been added—in several of the villages—about five to ten years later—and these begin to show the coarser mouldings and heavier details of the Greek influence, although the proportions and appearance have hardly begun as yet to show the change. But the houses built after that date exhibit less feeling for interest of detail; are larger and less interesting in composition and grouping; and show, beside, a tendency to abandon the smaller five and six room individual units, for the larger tenements of six, eight or ten family units. They are spaced more regularly along the streets; and the earlier habit of arranging them in row after row, back from the main street, spaced far apart, among groves of trees, with the service sheds and privies of from two to four cottages grouped into one structure, is abandoned for the less interesting monotonies of a more mechanized method and manner of development.

Of course, the "lay of the land" has much to do with the interest of certain groups, as at Hope itself. Here the street runs at a greater distance from the stream, there being three rows of cottages, arranged "in echelon," one behind the other, with the door-yards of the first row crowded close along behind the fencing upon the very margin of the street. All the smaller cottages are upon the side of the street running down hill to the stream; and across the street, where the land pitches more steeply upward, are a row of larger buildings, originally for four and six families, sometimes with the second story entered from the higher level of the land at the rear, thus saving the space given in other cottages in the line, to the staircase necessary to run from the front door up to the common landing upon the floor above.

Hope and Fiskeville are contiguous, with their centers hardly a quarter mile apart, and the smaller cottages in both villages are almost exactly alike, mostly belonging to the first or second period of building in the mill valley. At Fiskeville is the very interesting larger house, shown in several pictures in this chapter. While the side staircase and entrance are of about the period of other buildings in this vicinity, it would appear that the house was taken over and enlarged some fifteen or twenty years later, which would be about the period of the front entrance and stairway, and the upper monitor and cupola. This building stands directly across the street from the original house of the mill owner, and the mill, both of which were burned some score or so of years ago. This house was adapted to the use of a physician maintaining a sanitarium, as some of the rear rooms were fitted for containing his patients, and the cupola was originally equipped with small drawers and cupboards all around under the window stools to keep his medicines, herbs, and other medical aids in orderly arrangement.

INTERLARKEN MILLS HOUSE, HARRIS, RHODE ISLAND

MILL COTTAGE, ARKWRIGHT, RHODE ISLAND

MILL COTTAGES, FISKEVILLE, RHODE ISLAND

MILL COTTAGES, FISKEVILLE, RHODE ISLAND

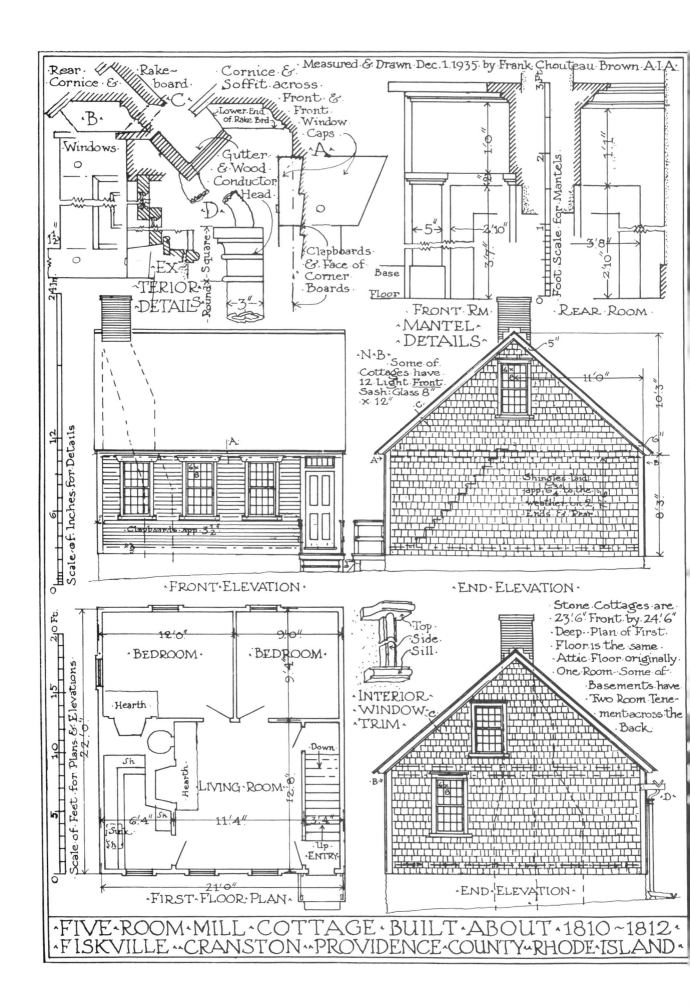

Measured & Drawn Dec. 1. 1935 by Frank Chouteau Brown A.I.A.

Rear Cornice & B — Rake-board — C — Cornice & Soffit across Front & Front Window Caps

Windows

Lower End of Rake Brd.

A

EX-TERIOR DETAILS

Gutter & Wood Conductor Head — D

Round × Square

3"

Clapboards & Face of Corner Boards

1 1/2"

24 in.

Scale of Inches for Details

FRONT · RM · MANTEL · DETAILS

Base
Floor

Foot Scale for Mantels

REAR · ROOM

N·B· Some of Cottages have 12 Light Front Sash: Glass 8" × 12"

FRONT · ELEVATION ·

Clapboards app 3 1/2"

· END · ELEVATION ·

11'·0"

10'·3"

8'·3"

Shingles laid app. 6" to the weather on 2 Ends & Rear.

Scale of Feet for Plans & Elevations

20 Ft.

BEDROOM 12'·0"

BEDROOM 9'·0"

Hearth

Hearth

LIVING · ROOM ·

6'·4"   11'·4"

Sink

Sh

Down

Up

ENTRY

12'·8"

22'·0"

21'·0"

· FIRST · FLOOR · PLAN ·

Top
Side
Sill

INTERIOR · WINDOW · TRIM ·

Stone Cottages are 23'·6" Front by 24'·6" Deep· Plan of First Floor is the same· Attic Floor originally One Room· Some of Basements have Two Room Tenement across the Back

· END · ELEVATION ·

·FIVE·ROOM·MILL·COTTAGE·BUILT·ABOUT·1810~1812·
·FISKVILLE·~CRANSTON·~PROVIDENCE·COUNTY·~RHODE·ISLAND·

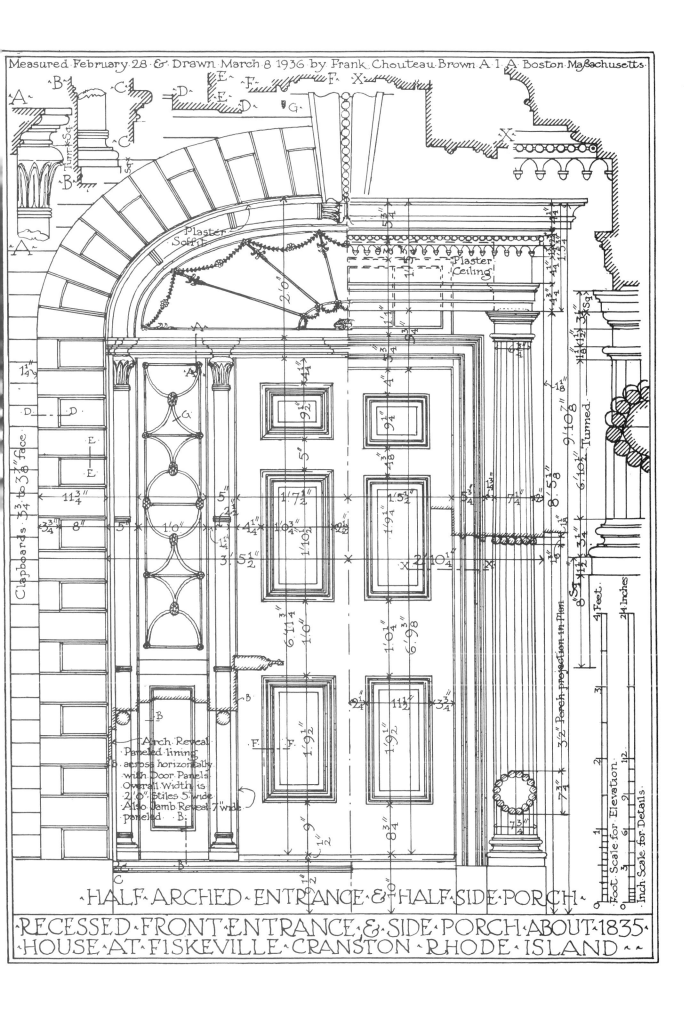

Measured February 28 & Drawn March 8 1936 by Frank Chouteau Brown A.I.A. Boston Massachusetts

Plaster Soffit

Plaster Ceiling

Arch Reveal
Paneled lining
5 across horizontally
with Door Panels
Overall Width is
2'.0" Stiles 5" wide.
Also Jamb Reveal 7" wide
Paneled.

Clapboards 5¾ to 3⅞" face

·HALF·ARCHED·ENTRANCE·&·HALF·SIDE·PORCH·

·RECESSED·FRONT·ENTRANCE·&·SIDE·PORCH·ABOUT·1835·
·HOUSE·AT·FISKEVILLE·CRANSTON·RHODE·ISLAND·~~

Foot Scale for Elevation.

Inch Scale for Details.

Side Porch

Porch Detail

TWO HOUSES AT FISKEVILLE, CRANSTON, RHODE ISLAND

HOUSE AT FISKEVILLE, CRANSTON, RHODE ISLAND

LONSDALE MILL COTTAGES, HOPE, RHODE ISLAND

LONSDALE MILL COTTAGES, HOPE, RHODE ISLAND

LONSDALE MILL HOUSE, HOPE, RHODE ISLAND

LONSDALE MILL COTTAGE, HOPE, RHODE ISLAND

LONSDALE MILL COTTAGE, HOPE, RHODE ISLAND

LONSDALE MILL COTTAGE, HOPE, RHODE ISLAND

COTTAGE OFF VILLAGE STREET, HOPE, RHODE ISLAND

Lincoln, Rhode Island

Text by
George W. Gardner
Photographs by
Arthur C. Haskell
Originally published in 1935 as White Pine Monograph
Volume XXI, Number 1

Original One-Room House Portion
ISRAEL ARNOLD HOUSE — c1700 — LINCOLN, RHODE ISLAND

SOME EARLY "SINGLE-ROOM HOUSES" OF LINCOLN, RHODE ISLAND

DESPITE the fact that the stimulus actuating most of the early settlers of New England in emigrating to this country was based upon their desire to secure religious as well as civil liberty; immediately they became established in the new land, they themselves began to set up forms of government no less rigid than those they had escaped. And they further appeared to feel no conscientious qualms in imposing their ideas and forms upon all those who came to live in their newly settled communities. And this was one of the several factors — and certainly not the least important among them — that soon caused the removal of individuals or groups from the first settlements, to seek out other locations for themselves — and so brought about the establishment of a number of what were, at first, the most remote colonies.

Among the earliest groups to detach themselves from the first settlements in the Massachusetts Bay Colony were a number of families from New Towne (now Cambridge, Massachusetts) who settled in Hartford, under the Rev. Thomas Hooker; while another group of people from Watertown settled Weathersfield, under John Talcot as leader — and still a third group, from Dorchester, established themselves at Windsor, also in what is now the state of Connecticut.

Meanwhile, Roger Williams had been forced to make his escape from Salem, Massachusetts, in the winter of 1635–1636, settling first in Seekonk (at East Providence, but still within the Massachusetts control, as that area was claimed by Plymouth), and then later — in order to avoid all possible controversy — moving across to the west side of the river, establishing himself where now is the city of Providence. The first houses there built were located near the present Baptist Church, which was built in 1775 on the site of the first Meeting House of Roger Williams.

Portsmouth (Rhode Island) was settled by Anne Hutchinson and others; following Coddington and Clarke, who had first settled there and then removed further to the south, to Newport — at a still safer distance from the militant Bay colonies! As usual, these first settlements were established either along the sea coast, especially where sheltered harbors or river mouths gave propitious locations; or along the larger rivers inland from the coast; or upon the shores of the many estuaries or deepcut bays and inlets with which the coast of Rhode Island, particularly, is lavishly indented.

Many of these early settlements were made in the southern portion of the state. In 1639 a trading post was set up at Cocumscussic (now Wickford), just after the outbreak of the Pequot War, in 1637. The King's Province, or Narragansett County, was also established, at the southwestern present border of Rhode Island; while the state itself secured its charter in 1663, and Williams died in 1683, after having firmly established a system of government that — unlike the Massachusetts settlements — made a definite division between Church and State.

With all this uncertainty of permanence, it can readily be seen that the early types of dwelling architecture were likely to have been of the simplest. And so it was that a "one-room house" plan became most characteristic of the first houses built in the woods and meadows of this country, that was to grow into a separate state, but had passed all its early years in an uncertain state of suspension between the colonies of Massachusetts Bay on the north, and the closely affiliated branch settlements to the west and south, that had been set up along the valley of the Connecticut by groups of people largely from the Massachusetts area.

The one-room house had usually one room only upon its first floor; and was a story and a half high,

even better known locally as the Stone Chimney House.

Within a comparatively small area upon the old road that still twists its way along the stream that widens into pond after pond—themselves the remains of old power sites, held in by old stone dams, in many instances now so overgrown with trees as hardly to be noted as artificial to the landscape—may still be found nearly a dozen old dwellings that once belonged to some member of the old Arnold family. In recent years some have become so changed that their old values and

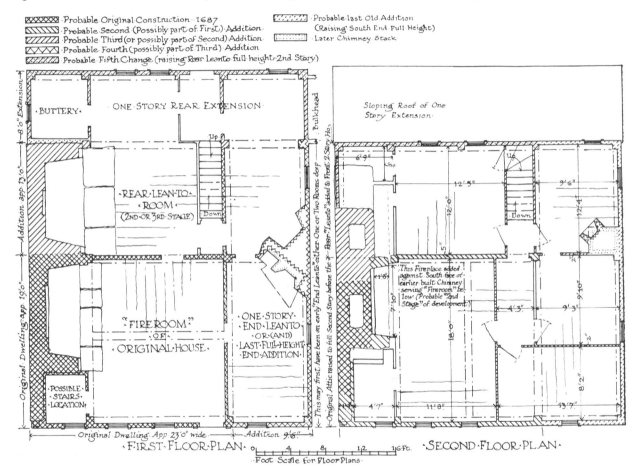

ELEAZER ARNOLD HOUSE (STONE CHIMNEY HOUSE), LINCOLN, RHODE ISLAND

with a one-room attic above. Some of the simplest dwellings had so low a roofridge that the area above the ceiling could only be used for storage. Sometimes, by aid of a ladder, it could be used as a sort of barracks for the children of a family. And then it might often be reached by a real stairway—and even perhaps boast of a small fireplace, all its own! Finally, a few examples probably may have had two full-height rooms, one over the other, with an attic above both. One of the most interesting and puzzling examples of this type is the Eleazer Arnold House at Lincoln, perhaps

interest have been lost; but the Eleazer Arnold House; although changed in many ways from its simple original, yet remains among the most picturesque survivals of the late seventeenth century structures to be seen in the region of the Providence Plantations.

An endeavor has been made to plot at least the most important changes that evidence themselves in the existing fabric of this old structure—as there are contradictory theories as to its origins and evolution into its present form. It now stands as it was restored a dozen or so years ago, through both local and New

One-Room House Part Built About 1687
ELEAZER ARNOLD HOUSE (STONE CHIMNEY HOUSE), LINCOLN, RHODE ISLAND

England interest. In the attic, the framing of a steep front gable still shows plainly, though it was not replaced when the last restoration was made. At that time, a number of smaller fireplaces and several old ovens were removed from the northeast corners of the two first-floor chimneys. The southern end of the present house was probably part of the last additions made in olden times; with the comparatively new brick chimney stack, that shows only in the rear views of the building. All the other changes must have been of very early date; made soon after the original portion of the house, dating from about 1687, was erected.

story fireplace, that occurs only in the room over the front section of the dwelling—and was unquestionably built against the south face of the already completed stone chimney serving the large fireplace of the room below.

That the room at the rear was built after the stonework of the westernmost fireplace was completed would appear probable from the fact that its chimney stonework does not align with the earlier chimney, and exhibits obvious adjustments made to fit it to the framing lines established by the older corner posts and the

East Elevation
ELEAZER ARNOLD HOUSE, LINCOLN, RHODE ISLAND

tion of the house, dating from about 1687, was erected.

This may have been one of the characteristic local one-room houses; of which the older ell portion of the Israel Arnold House nearby furnishes an indubitable example. In that event, the present small closet at the northeast corner of the building may have contained a steep staircase to the attic above. (It is of just about the size and proportions of the staircase space in the Israel Arnold House ell nearby.) Another contributary piece of evidence may be found in the second-

newer chimney girder framing into them at the second-floor level. On the other hand, it may be that the one-room plan of the original section was two stories high, either in its original, or in nearly as early a second state—and that the rear room on the first floor was built to come within a rear lean-to, whose possible outlines have been dotted across the northwest corner in the cross section drawing.

In that event, the oddly framed eight-foot-wide addition made across the entire back of the building—with its northeast corner closet, probably the buttery

ELEAZER ARNOLD HOUSE, LINCOLN, RHODE ISLAND

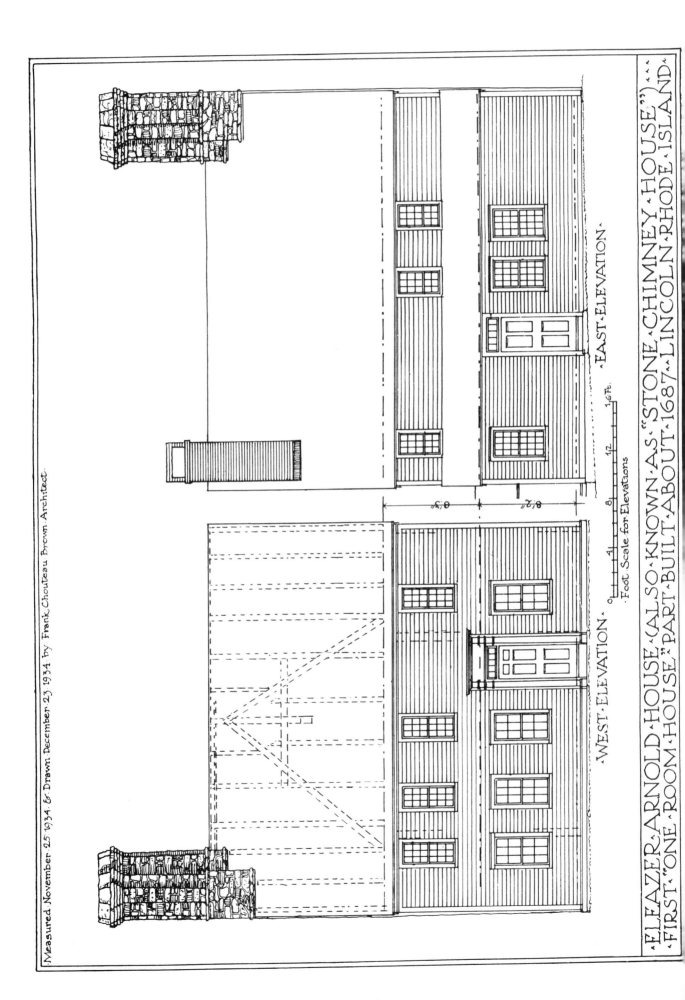

Measured November 25 1934 & Drawn December 23 1934 by Frank Chouteau Brown Architect.

·WEST·ELEVATION·

·EAST·ELEVATION·

0'.3"

8'.2"

0   2   4   8   12   16 Ft.

·Foot·Scale·for·Elevations·

·ELEAZER·ARNOLD·HOUSE·(ALSO·KNOWN·AS·"STONE·CHIMNEY·HOUSE")···
·FIRST·"ONE·ROOM·HOUSE"·PART·BUILT·ABOUT·1687··LINCOLN·RHODE·ISLAND·

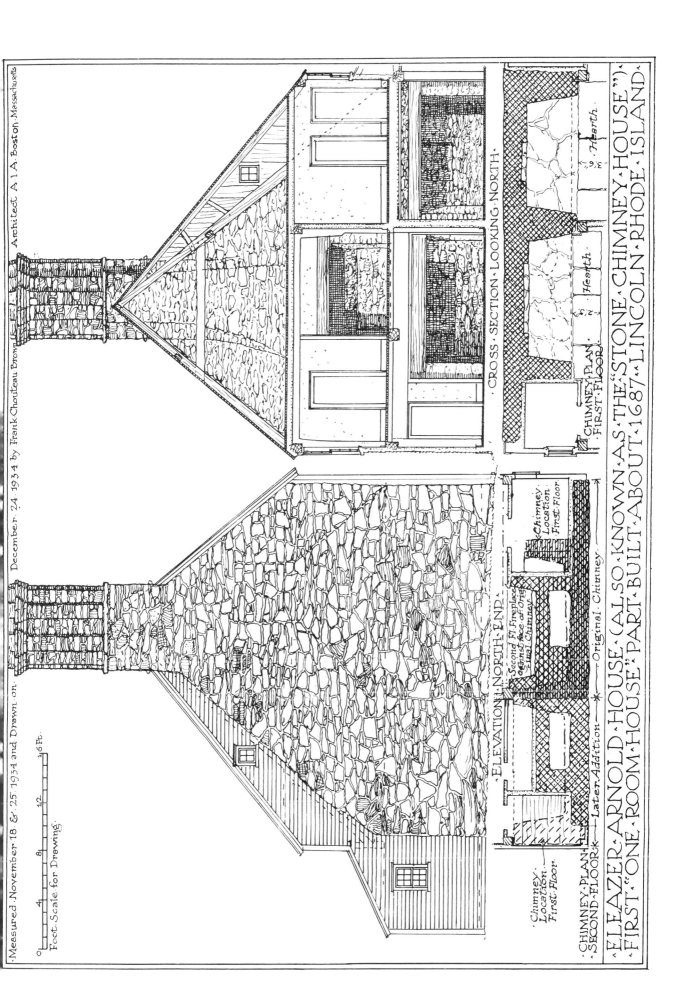

·Measured·November·18·&·25·1934·and·Drawn·on· · · December·24·1934·by·Frank·Chouteau·Brown· · · Architect·A·I·A·Boston·Massachusetts

·Foot·Scale·for·Drawing·

0 · 4 · 8 · 12 · 16 Ft.

·CROSS·SECTION·LOOKING·NORTH·

·Hearth·

3'·6"

·Hearth·

·6"

·CHIMNEY·PLAN·
·FIRST·FLOOR·

·ELEVATION·NORTH·END·

·Second·Ft·Fireplace·
·against·face·of·Orig·
·inal·Chimney·

·Chimney·
·Location·
·First·Floor·

·Chimney·
·Location·
·First·Floor·

·CHIMNEY·PLAN·
·SECOND·FLOOR·

·Later·Addition·— — —·Original·Chimney·

·ELEAZER·ARNOLD·HOUSE·(ALSO·KNOWN·AS·THE·"STONE·CHIMNEY·HOUSE")·
·FIRST·"ONE·ROOM·HOUSE"·PART·BUILT·ABOUT·1687·LINCOLN·RHODE·ISLAND·

ELEAZER ARNOLD HOUSE (STONE CHIMNEY HOUSE)—1687—LINCOLN, RHODE ISLAND

West End Elevation, One-Room House Portion
ISRAEL ARNOLD HOUSE — c1700 — LINCOLN, RHODE ISLAND

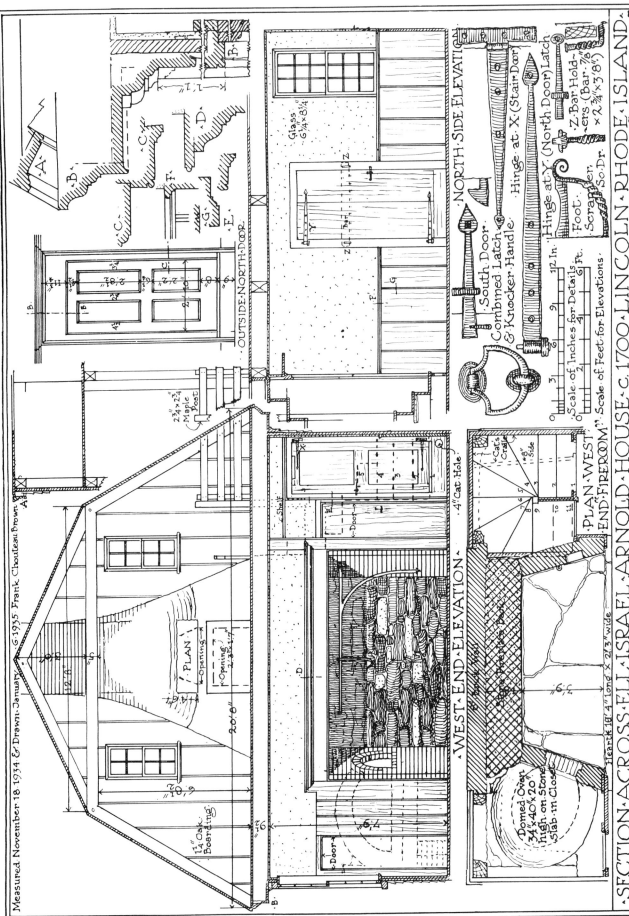

Measured November 18 1934 & Drawn January 6 1935 Frank Chouteau Brown

·OUTSIDE·NORTH·DOOR·

·NORTH·SIDE·ELEVATION·

Glass· 6¼"×8¼"

Hinge at X (Stair Door)
South Door.
Combined Latch & Knocker Handle·
Hinge at·Y· (North Door) Latch

Foot· Z·Bar·Hold-
Scraper· ers· (Bar· ⅞"
× 2¾"×3 8")

·Scale·of·Inches·for·Details·
·Scale·of·Feet·for·Elevations·

2¾"×2¾" Maple Post

Shelf

4" Cat Hole

Cat's Crate
1'-8" Side

·PLAN·WEST
·END·FIREROOM·

·WEST·END·ELEVATION·

Domed Oven 34"×40"×20" high·on·Stone Slab·in·Closet

Hearth 10'-4" long × 2'3" wide

·Opening· 2'-3"×1'-7"

·PLAN·
·Opening·
7'-9½"×4'4"

20'-8"

12'-6"

1¼" Oak Boarding

20'-9"

·SECTION·ACROSS·ELI·ISRAEL·ARNOLD·HOUSE·c.1700·LINCOLN·RHODE·ISLAND·
·ORIGINAL·ONE·ROOM·HOUSE·PORTION·SHOWING·NORTH·SIDE·&·WEST·END·OF·FIRE·ROOM·

ANOTHER ARNOLD HOUSE, LINCOLN, RHODE ISLAND

—may have been put on at the time the present deeper second story, and newer lean-to rafters, now appearing in the attic leaning against the older roof timbers from the ridge eastward, were put in place; or it may have been a widening added at quite another period; perhaps at about the time the house was made longer on its street face by the newer southern end; which was apparently erected before—or at the same time—that the front gable was framed into the old roof timbering on the west front. Some of the windows are old, and some of later date also appear. The front entrance and doorway belong to the early nineteenth

western side still remains much as it was originally built. This fortunately contains the huge fireplace with brick wings and stone back that shows in photograph and drawing; flanked on the north by the old staircase to the attic space above and on the south by a closet space, most of which is taken up by the huge three-foot-long domed oven, that has been built within it, upon a stone slab set sixteen inches above the floor. The stone fireplace back has been backed again by a wall of brick that shows outside; and the gambrel roof given the old house indicates both its (comparatively) late date and a probable need or desire for larger capac-

ANOTHER ARNOLD HOUSE, LINCOLN, RHODE ISLAND

century; and may not mark the location of the first doorway. The more one studies the arrangement of this building in its present state, the more possible variants in the various stages of its development appear; most of which will probably always remain in the realm of conjecture!

Whatever the original Stone Chimney House plan may have been, there can be no doubt but that the present ell of the Israel Arnold House nearby still stands in almost the identical condition in which it existed from before 1700 up to the time the larger present house was added to it, some years later. The closing of windows and opening of doors in its eastern wall must have been occasioned by the addition of the later house at that side of the original structure; but its

ity of the second-floor space. The chimney tops of both houses have been changed and the chimneys stuccoed; but the old fire room remains in its identical original condition, with the staircase and closets, and even the old "cat's cradle" with its four-inch circular entrance, appears in the first step riser showing below the door at the right of the fireplace.

The larger house has simple finish, and a characteristic stairway, along with a type of mantel treatment that is representative of some of the local traditions, including even the cupboard or set of open shelves—usually with a sloping back—that often appears hereabouts, in the space over the fire opening—whereas northern New England more frequently supplies instead a large panel in the over-mantel.

In the same general neighborhood are to be found two other existing records of this early type of structure. One, just off a newly widened thoroughfare, extending toward the north from Providence, is now no more than a store shed in a farmyard group. But little of its old framework remains, only one or two of the rafters, a corner post or so; a bit of old shingled wall, a few small areas of old split laths and plaster — *and* the chimney, with its stone back showing through the old end-wall of the building! The old brick domed oven and stonework of the fireplace show clearly its age;

type. Nevertheless, a considerable part of its existing structure — including the odd fireplace and chimney — must be original enough to permit its inclusion within this group of a fast-vanishing type of local early dwelling, for what evidence and interest it may still supply. Little is known about its history. It would appear that there may have been an upper floor across the building at one time, from the single piece that still remains along each side plate, under the ends of the sloping rafters. No trace of staircase may now be found. It may have been merely either a permanent

CAPTAIN JOHN JENKS HOUSE, LINCOLN, RHODE ISLAND

while the upper portion, built of brick above the fire opening, may now be seen above the cross ceiling pieces to the under side of the roof boarding. About all the old finish, and wall boarding, have disappeared; and the rest may vanish almost any day — unless means soon may be taken to preserve it! This is a type where the attic space could only have been used for storage, as it is barely five feet high under the roof peak.

In the old Fireplace House, in Lincoln Woods, which stands in the shadow of another Arnold house, dating from before 1750; the interior also lies open to view. But this house has been in some part "restored," as appears obvious from any close study of its framework and enclosing walls, and therefore it is not to be entirely accepted as an authentic example of its

wall ladder, or a removable central one. The very small and low brick fireplace in the side of the left stone cheek of the larger one, is supposed to have been used for the drying of spinning flax, in which case a small room may have been partitioned off at the end of the present space, to have been used for that purpose.

No oven now remains; but quite a large hole in the stonework at the rear of the fireplace back shows where either a domed oven outside the fireplace corner may have been made — or it may have been, as some believe, an *outside* door into an inner corner oven — in which case there may at one time have been an outer summer kitchen against that end wall of the present building.

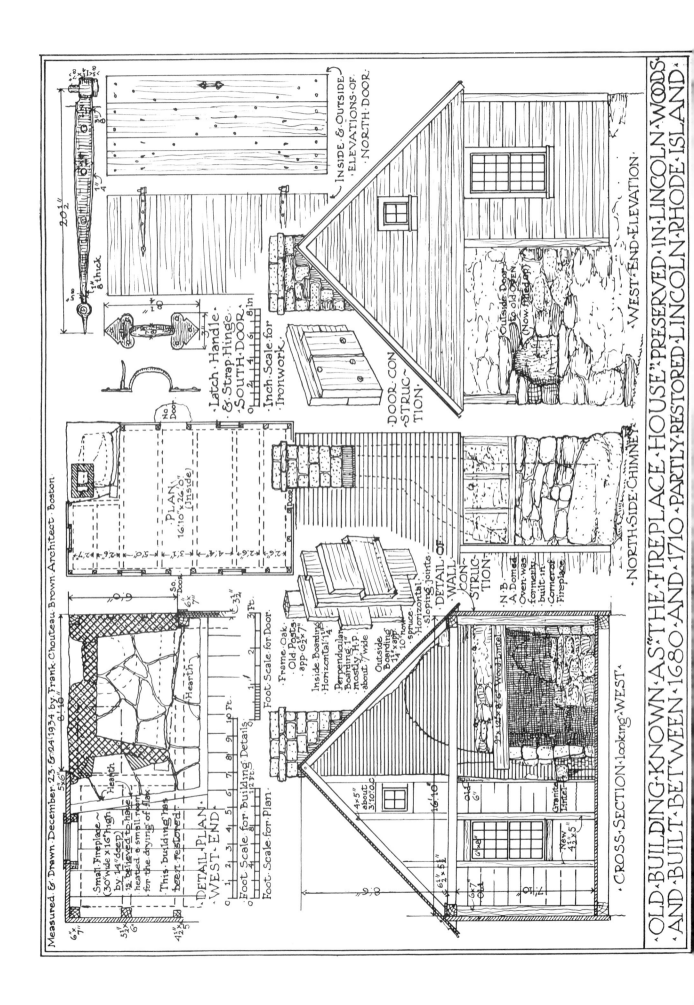

Measured · & · Drawn · December · 23 · & · 24 · 1934 · by · Frank · Chouteau · Brown · Architect · Boston ·

Small · Fireplace ~
(30"wide x 16"high
by 14"deep)
is · believed · to · have ·
heated · a · small · room ·
for · the · drying · of · flax ·

This · building · has ·
been · restored ·

Hearth

· DETAIL · PLAN ·
· WEST · END ·

Foot · Scale · for · Building · Details ·

Foot · Scale · for · Plan ·

· PLAN ·
16'10" x 26'-0"
(Inside)

No
Door

So.
Door

· Inside · & · Outside ·
· ELEVATIONS · OF ·
· NORTH · DOOR ·

· Latch · Handle ·
& · Strap · Hinge ·
· SOUTH · DOOR ·

Inch · Scale · for · Ironwork ·

1" thick

20½"

· DOOR · CON~
· STRUC~
· TION ·

Frame · Oak ·
Old · Posts ·
app · 6½ x 7"

Inside · Boarding ·
Horizontal · 1¼" ·

Perpendicular ·
Boarding · 1" ·
mostly, H.P. ·
about ¾"wide ·

Outside ·
Boarding ·
1¼" x app ·
10" now ·
spruce ·
horizontal ·
sloping · joints ·

· DETAIL · OF ·
· WALL · CON~
· STRUC~
· TION ·

N.B.
A · Domed ·
Oven · was ·
formerly ·
built · in ·
Corner · of ·
Fireplace ·

Foot · Scale · for · Door ·

· CROSS · SECTION · looking · WEST ·

4 x 5"
about
3' 10" O.C.

16'10"

Old
6"

9" x 14" x 8'-6" Wood · Lintel ·

6'-1" x 5½"
Old

6' 7"
Old

New
4¼ x 5

Granite
Lintel

9' 0"

· NORTH · SIDE · CHIMNEY ·

Outside · Door ·
to · old · OVEN ·
(Now · filled · in) ·

· WEST · END · ELEVATION ·

· OLD · BUILDING · KNOWN · AS · "THE · FIREPLACE · HOUSE" · PRESERVED · IN · LINCOLN · WOODS ·
· AND · BUILT · BETWEEN · 1680 · AND · 1710 · PARTLY · RESTORED · LINCOLN · RHODE · ISLAND ·

ISRAEL ARNOLD HOUSE—c1700—LINCOLN, RHODE ISLAND

A Providence Georgian Mansion

Text by
Frank Chouteau Brown
Photographs by
Arthur C. Haskell
Originally published in 1936 as White Pine Monograph
Volume XXII, Number 1

PERRY HOUSE, PROVIDENCE, RHODE ISLAND

A PROVIDENCE GEORGIAN MANSION:
THE HOUSE FOUNDED
BY JOHN BROWN, ESQ., 1786

LOOKING south down Narragansett Bay, from the sloping hillsides surrounding the business center, Providence—now the second largest of New England cities—is situated in one of the most ideal locations along the Atlantic coast. This encircling grouping of low hills (some of which have now ceased to exist) was responsible for its present somewhat confused city plan; as the locations of the older main roadways leading out of or into the city radiated along the valleys lying between these hills. While the civic center (Market Square, with the old Market House of 1773 still standing—if somewhat changed) and business district of the city started upon the swampish meadow that originally supplied rich and abundant pasturage to the cows of the first landed "proprietors" (thirty-eight in number, a few years after the settlement), it was fortunate that the removal of some of the hills to the westward of this area permitted the business district to expand in that direction. Some of the material thus obtained was used to fill and raise the meadow, and extend its area southward along the lines of the present day docks; while Weybosset Hill was entirely used by Mr. Thomas Staples in his brick industry, always a favorite material in Providence, the increased use of which was especially favored after the fire of 1758, which brought about the purchase of a "fire-engine," as well as a law requiring every citizen to keep two fire buckets always ready at hand!

This meadow had been separated from the steeply rising slope of what is now known as College Hill, by the confluence of the Mooshasuch and Woonasquatucket Rivers, whose waters are now almost entirely covered—and the first Towne Street (later becoming North and South Main Street) extended along the eastern bank of this waterway, and still retains many important old structures, facing toward the west.

Among the early settlers was the Rev. Chad Brown, first pastor of the First Baptist Church, which was organized in 1638 by Roger Williams and others—being the first society organized in America and the second oldest in the world—although they had no regular meeting house for some time, but met at the homes of the members. Between 1715 and 1720, one of his descendants, Nathaniel Brown, began building ships in his yards just across the Weybosset River, about where Washington and Exchange streets now are; and here sloops, schooners and brigs—the largest not exceeding 100 tons!—were built for use in the coastal trade, and even in the rapidly growing business then developing between the northern colonies and the West Indies.

Meanwhile, two of Chad Brown's great-grandsons, James and Obadiah, started a business together about 1733, and by 1736 had four sloops employed in the West India trade. James married Hope, a granddaughter of Pardon Tillinghast, who had built the first warehouse and wharf in Providence in 1679, about where Transit and South streets come together; and by 1739 he had died, leaving four sons, Nicholas, Joseph, John, and Moses; all of whom were associated in business from about 1763 to 1773, when Moses Brown retired, joined the Friends Meeting the following year and, in 1790, financed Samuel Slater, a young Englishman, in perfecting cotton spinning machinery in his mill at Pawtucket. This was the start in Rhode Island of the mill business that has since flourished along the Blackstone and Pawtucket Rivers. Joseph retired from the firm during the Revolution, and Nicholas and John continued until about 1782.

Of all the four brothers, Moses is perhaps the best

known; both from his long life (he was born Sept. 23, 1738, and died Sept. 6, 1836) and his many interests and public-spirited acts. But John, Nicholas, and Joseph were also well and widely known in all the industrial and business life of the community, and especially as public benefactors and leaders in its civic improvements and municipal developments.

In the years between 1732 and 1784, Providence-built and owned vessels had carried on a considerable slave trade with African ports — but most of its business had been with the West Indies. In 1787 John Brown started trade direct with the East Indies and China; from wharves located on what has ever since been known as India Point. The first ship built by him especially for the China and East India trade was named the *Gen. Washington*, sailed on Dec. 24, 1787, from Providence, and returned July 5, 1789, after logging 32,758 miles, with a cargo valued at $99,848. This, also, was a small vessel; but in January of 1791, Brown and Francis had built and launched for that trade by far the largest ship ever to sail from that port, the *Pres. Washington*, of the enormous size of 950 tons!

But John Brown's participation in the plot against the *Gaspee*, an eight-gun schooner that, along with the sloop-of-war *Beaver*, had been stationed in Narragansett Bay to enforce the collection of the revenues for the Crown, should be mentioned. While in chase of the sloop Hannah, the *Gaspee* ran aground on Namquit — now known as Gaspee Point, below Pawtucket — and on the evening of June 9, 1772, John Brown provided eight longboats, carrying the Providence men from the wharf opposite the Sabin house, at 124 South Main Street, where plans for the raid had been completed, to the successful capture and destruction of the British schooner.

Besides his interests in shipping and importing, John Brown had investments in the Hope Furnaces; was a member of the group organizing the first bank in Providence (when the enterprise was initiated in 1784 there were only four in all the colonies, New York, Baltimore, Boston, and Philadelphia) in 1791.

On March 27, 1791, John Brown laid the corner stone of University Hall, built to house the new Baptist College that had been started in Warren a few years previously (1764–1765). The influence of all four brothers had been employed to secure the removal of Rhode Island College, as it was then called, to Providence; and in 1804, following a large gift by Nicholas Brown the second — son of the Nicholas of the four brothers — all of whom had been generous benefactors of the institution, the name was changed to Brown University. John Brown died in 1803.

In 1700 Providence had a population of about 1500. By the end of the century it had grown to 7614; but though the city had fortunately escaped damage from raids by the British — such as had not been the case with its near neighbors, Warren and Bristol — during the Revolution; by the end of that war, its trade had suffered such interruption that the city had lost much of its former prosperity. Nevertheless, soon after a wave of house building started along the slope of College Hill, and especially upon the newly laid out Benefit Street — which had been built in 1756, after several years of discussion, as it was to cut across all the hillside lots of the original proprietors, and unfortunately at just about the locations of their family burial grounds.

One of the most imposing of the new dwellings built on the slope of hill overlooking the wharves and harbor was completed by John Brown in 1786, from plans drawn by his brother Joseph, who died before it was completed, at a time when the total population of Providence was only about 6000 persons! It is known that Joseph Brown, in 1773 or earlier, had been appointed to make a study of plans for the First Baptist Church, along with Mr. James Sumner, a master workman then well known both in Boston and Providence, and Jonathan Hammond, a carpenter and joiner of the latter place. The present church edifice was completed in 1775; and the design is believed to have been taken from James Gibbs' *Book of Architecture, containing Designs of Buildings and Ornaments,* London, 1728; and something of the knowledge and experience Joseph Brown had then obtained undoubtedly was expended upon the design of the house built by his brother — as is evident from any study of the details of its design.

Fortunately, the successive owners of this dwelling have had the discernment to preserve its old qualities, in which they have been much assisted by the sturdy integrity and thoroughness with which the structure originally had been built. Changes have been made, but principally upon the rear of the building; in extending its service facilities; or in the replacement and improvement of its conveniences — or the final perfection and repair of its decorations and details.

Therefore, the main portion retains all its original dignity and effect, seen either from the entrance front or the ampler spaces of its westerly side. Within doors, the main rooms — so far as their finish is concerned — remain much as they were originally built. In the library new bookcases have been added; here and there a doorway has been changed or moved; some alterations have been made about the vestibule and entrance; but mantels and doorways, dados and cornices (if not always floors and ceilings) still show the beautiful workmanship of the old craftsmen; the lustre and polish of old mahogany; the delicacy of modeled plaster ornament on ceilings or hard putty moulding and carving on mantels or door caps; all of a skill that it is difficult to realize could belong to the early years of so small a community and so young a nation. And as to the date, we have better information than the usual local rumor, or the dubious wording of old deeds. The matter is made integral with the structure. For, proud evidently of his work and pains, the stone lintel over a rear doorway displays, in lettering cut boldly upon it, "THIS HOUSE FOUNDED BY JOHN BROWN, Esq., 1786."

Detail of Street Façade
JOHN BROWN HOUSE—1786—PROVIDENCE, RHODE ISLAND

JOHN BROWN HOUSE—1786—BENEFIT STREET, PROVIDENCE, RHODE ISLAND

JOHN BROWN HOUSE—1786—BENEFIT STREET, PROVIDENCE, RHODE ISLAND

West Front Doorway
JOHN BROWN HOUSE — 1786 — PROVIDENCE, RHODE ISLAND

Street Front Doorway
JOHN BROWN HOUSE — 1786 — PROVIDENCE, RHODE ISLAND

Hall
JOHN BROWN HOUSE—1786—PROVIDENCE, RHODE ISLAND

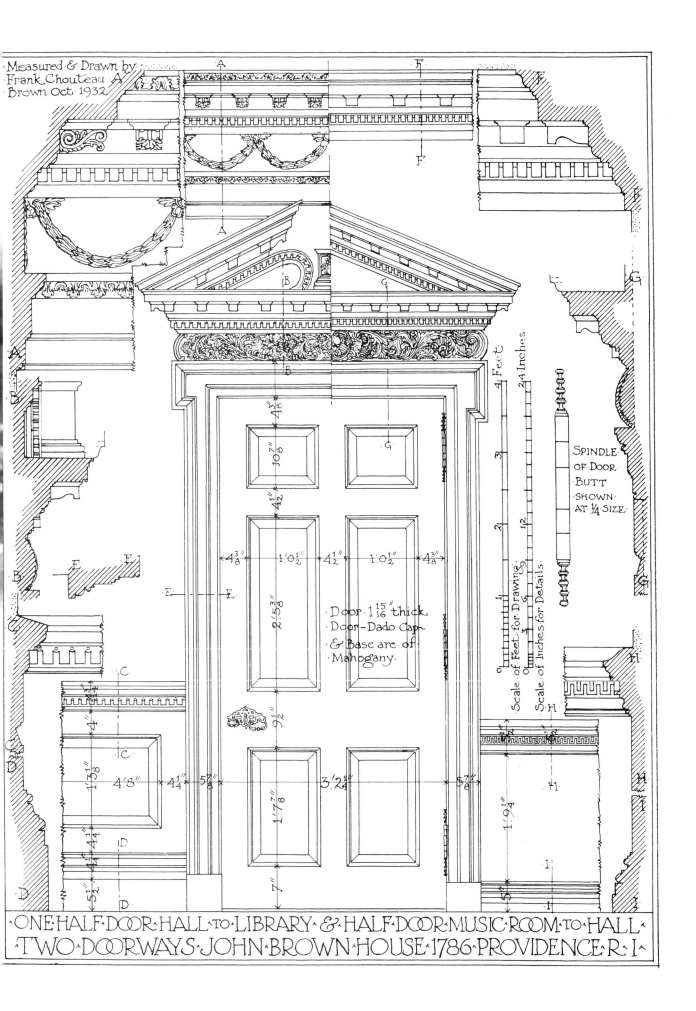

Measured & Drawn by Frank Chouteau A. Brown Oct. 1932

SPINDLE OF DOOR BUTT SHOWN AT ¼ SIZE.

Door 1 15/16" thick
Door–Dado Cap & Base are of Mahogany.

4 Feet

24 Inches.

Scale of Feet for Drawing.

Scale of Inches for Details.

·ONE·HALF·DOOR·HALL·TO·LIBRARY· & ·HALF·DOOR·MUSIC·ROOM·TO·HALL·
·TWO·DOORWAYS·JOHN·BROWN·HOUSE·1786·PROVIDENCE·R·I·

Detail of Doorway, Music Room to Hall

Detail of Doorway, Hall to Library

JOHN BROWN HOUSE—1786—PROVIDENCE, RHODE ISLAND

Detail of Doorway in Hall

Detail of Doorway, Parlor to Hall

JOHN BROWN HOUSE—1786—PROVIDENCE, RHODE ISLAND

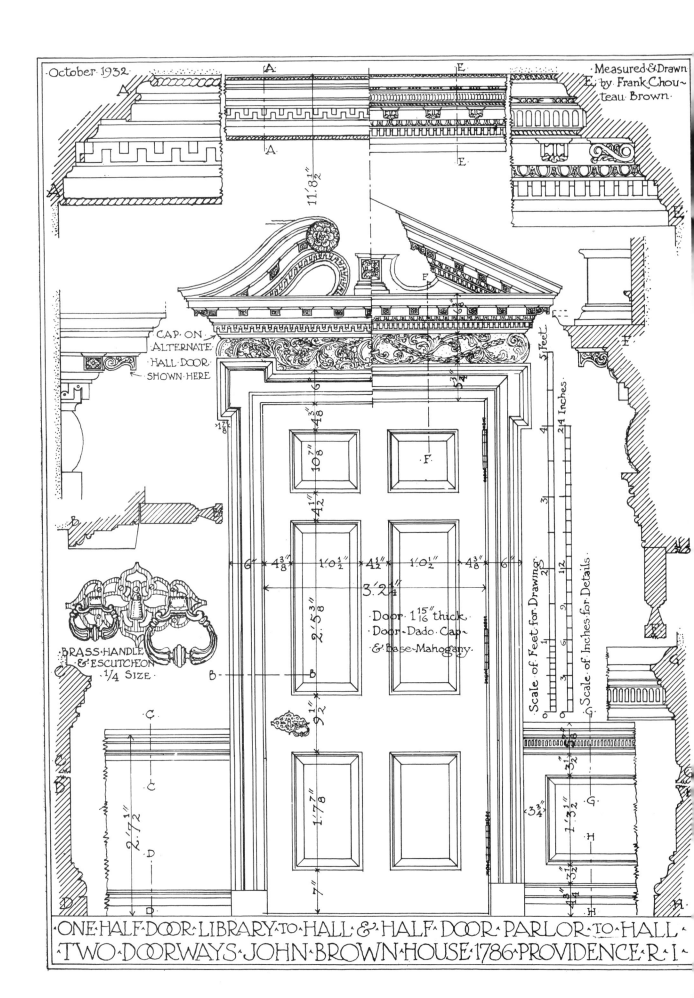

October 1932

Measured & Drawn by Frank Chou~ teau Brown

CAP ON ALTERNATE HALL DOOR SHOWN HERE

BRASS HANDLE & ESCUTCHEON 1/4 SIZE

Door 1 15/16" thick
Door~Dado~Cap~ & Base~Mahogany.

Scale of Feet for Drawing.

Scale of Inches for Details.

ONE·HALF·DOOR·LIBRARY·TO·HALL·&·HALF·DOOR·PARLOR·TO·HALL·
TWO·DOORWAYS·JOHN·BROWN·HOUSE·1786·PROVIDENCE·R·I·

Parlor
JOHN BROWN HOUSE — 1786 — PROVIDENCE, RHODE ISLAND

Music Room
JOHN BROWN HOUSE—1786—PROVIDENCE, RHODE ISLAND

Music Room
JOHN BROWN HOUSE — 1786 — PROVIDENCE, RHODE ISLAND

SCALE·FOR·DETAILS

·FIRST·F
SCAL
FOR·PL

23'·4"

45'·6"

30'·0"

21'·0"

23'·4"

DETAI

·F R O N T·E

T H E · B R I
·A N N A P O L I